Sarah Ivens in the Editor-in-C[...]
America. She has written for *Tatler*, *GQ*, *Cosmopolitan*,
Marie Claire, *Men's Health*, *InStyle*, the *Daily Mail* and
the *Mirror*. She is a born and bred Londoner who now
lives in New York City.

Sarah's first four books, *A Modern Girl's Guide to Getting
Hitched*, *A Modern Girl's Guide to Dynamic Dating*,
A Modern Girl's Guide to Etiquette and *The Bride's Guide
to Unique Weddings* are also published by Piatkus.

A Modern Girl's Guide
to Networking

Contents

Dedication

To my Essex Girls, Kent University Birds and Media
Darlings ... Good friends are like stars – you don't always
see them, but you know they are always there!

Visit the Piatkus website!

Piatkus publishes a wide range of bestselling fiction and non-fiction, including books on health, mind body & spirit, sex, self-help, cookery, biography and the paranormal.

If you want to:
- read descriptions of our popular titles
- buy our books over the internet
- take advantage of our special offers
- enter our monthly competition
- learn more about your favourite Piatkus authors

VISIT OUR WEBSITE AT: www.piatkus.co.uk

First published in 2007 by
Piatkus Books Limited
5 Windmill Street
London WIT 2JA

e-mail: info@piatkus.co.uk

The moral right of the author has been asserted

A catalogue record for this book is available from the British Library

ISBN 0 7499 2758 5

Edited by Jan Cutler
Illustrations by Megan Hess
Text design by Paul Saunders

This book has been printed on paper manufactured with respect for the environment using wood from managed sustainable resources

Printed and bound in Great Britain by Clays Ltd, St Ives plc

A Modern Girl's Guide to Networking

How to win friends and influence people –
from the office to the party, from the boardroom
to the bedroom

SARAH IVENS

PIATKUS

Acknowledgements

Thanks to Alice Davis for developing such a much-needed book in the Modern Girl series, and to everyone at Piatkus for not forgetting about me once I left Blighty. Lovely cover, Megan Hess – you illustrator extraordinaire, you!

The last year has been a tough one for me but I've had the loveliest family in the world to get me through it. Mum, Dad, James, William, Grandma, Auntie Joan, Auntie Joyce and Debs – you mean the world to me.

Special thanks to the 'old' friends who know me inside and out: Claire, Hayley, Andrea, Rose, Donna, Excella, Emma, Jade, Liz, Mel, Flavia, Julia, Carolyn, Kate, Claire I., Hollie, James, David, Billy and JCJ.

Rob, Ruth Juliet, Katie, Mel, Ian, Tim, Lara, Vincent, Matt and the team at *OK!*: my new friends Alex, Jason, Felipe and Gaby who have made New York feel like home and Los Angeles feel a bit more normal. How would I have survived the last two years without you?

Finally, for Ben – the most natural networker I know... and the nicest one too!

Introduction

IT IS A VERY RARE human being (spectacular or stupid) who wishes to make life harder for him or herself. Most of us wish to do what we can to be happy, successful, popular, rich and content with minimum effort and fuss. Yes, we put in extra time at the office to make our boss happy, or go to the gym when spring arrives and bikini weather is just around the corner, but generally we'd rather be sipping a cocktail on a sunlounger than slogging our guts out.

This is where networking comes in. The right kind of networking can make your life that little bit easier and your path on the road to riches and respect just that little bit smoother. Modern networking is a must-have combination of good manners, confidence and business know-how. You'll learn how to master these three skills in the forthcoming chapters ... and once you have them, doors will start opening.

Friends and colleagues can never believe it now, but I used to be terribly shy. I was the kid at the back of the class who longed to put her hand up to answer a teacher's question but knew she'd stumble on the words so kept her mouth shut. I longed to join the choir but thought I wasn't good enough. If someone said a handsome boy in my class liked me, I'd go bright red in the cheeks and studiously ignore him for the rest of the school term.

Every teenager goes through this awkward stage – how I cringe now, looking back – but you don't have to suffer from these insecurities for ever (not publicly, anyway).

Setting my heart on a career in journalism, I knew I'd have to educate myself and have more faith in my abilities. I started to choose friends who would instil confidence into me, I listened to bosses who would nurture me, and I observed those who had been successful while clinging on to the values that I admired: kindness, loyalty and a sense of fun. Luckily, I discovered lots of worthy role models.

I didn't change overnight, but gradually, slowly, I noticed I could attend a meeting and hold my own, or when introduced to a senior manager could talk sense. I could even give presentations in front of 50 or more people without blushing! I learned how to increase my confidence and communicate better – two major networking needs.

Now, people can't believe I was ever that quiet little girl, intimidated by classroom bullies or mean bosses – although inside I'm still the same, of course.

My favourite poem, one which I believe means a lot when thinking of networking, and how to handle different situations and different people, is entitled 'If', by Rudyard Kipling . To paraphrase, Kipling insists that if you can walk with kings but still get along with your own people and those less privileged than yourself then you will be a well-rounded individual. How true. A good networker feels as at home with an A-list celebrity as the waiter in her favourite restaurant. A good networker can talk to all, befriend everyone and minimise awkward silences with natural charm and an ability to make small talk.

So, here we go: in ten chapters you'll learn some invaluable tips, hear some interesting stories and understand how to increase your chances of success – both professionally and personally with *A Modern Girl's Guide to Networking*. Hey, who said you couldn't have it all ... and more ... without the 1980s shoulder pads?

Chapter One

Necessary networking for an easy life

IT'S IMPORTANT TO NOTE that this book is called *A Modern Girl's Guide to Networking*. This isn't the same kind of book that would have been written for our senior sisters in the 1960s, or even the 1980s, where there were still so many sexism battles to be won both in the workplace and in society. Of course, there are still great inequalities (men earn on average 30 per cent more than women doing an equivalent job, for example) and glass ceilings to smash, but at least women are in a place where they can fight. We've got through the door, now we just need to make ourselves at home.

What is networking?

Networking is the art of skilfully and subtly building contacts and making new friends. It's not about sending out a group email when you've lost your job and asking those people who you've been too busy to speak to for years to do you a favour. It's about making alliances and connections of mutual benefit. And networking isn't just about getting a move up the corporate ladder, it's also about long-term planning and knowing what's going on in the world in general.

When are you networking?

You are networking every time you leave the house. You don't have to be wearing a badge with your name on it, or furiously shaking hands with Japanese businessmen to be networking. However, it's too obvious if you just begin to talk to your successful brother-in-law after you've been made redundant! In fact, you're networking (but without thinking about it) when you are:

◆ Chatting to people on Internet sites.

◆ Learning new skills at your local college or sports centre.

◆ Going away for the weekend with friends, and their friends.

◆ Volunteering in the local community.

◆ Throwing your child a birthday party and saying that other parents are welcome to come, too.

◆ Catching up with your neighbours.

◆ Attending a singles' event.

◆ Joining a club or society.

◆ Subscribing to educational or vocational courses.

If you're a mum, you're networking when you are chatting to other mothers at the school gates. If you're a secretary, you're networking when you are being polite to the post-room boy. If you're a doctor, you're networking when you share a drink with a journalist on holiday. The truth is we all network all day long (or we should be). In the simplest sense of the word, networking is no more than being sociable – both socially interested and interesting. Of course, it's how you manipulate this interaction that makes it valuable.

How can it improve your life?

For a start, networking improves your confidence: the more strangers you chat to and get on with, the better you will feel about yourself and your ability to meet new people. Networking will also improve your social life: the wider your friendship circle, the more diverse and interesting events will fill up your calendar. And, of course, the biggest use for networking is to realise your career ambitions. It's an interesting US statistic that 80 per cent of job vacancies are never advertised, but filled through networking (be it through word of mouth, industry social events or the not-so-admirable nepotism!). Networking, by its most basic definition, means casting your net wide to all opportunities – and having the skills to make the most of them.

Does being a networker mean becoming a smarmy schmoozer?

There is a certain image of a successful networker being a rather overbearing lick-arse! Don't fulfil this stereotype. At all times think good manners and sociability, not fake charm and cupboard love. People see through it. There is a fantastic quote from a US Congressman called J.C. Watts that makes lots of sense when learning to become a better networker: 'Character is doing the right thing when nobody is looking.' What I believe he is saying is that it's easy to be full of fake smiles and fawning when you're trying to win a new contract or client, but it's your basic good character that will keep them with you and that wins true respect. The best networkers I know are the ones who aren't obviously at an event to slime up to people for money or contacts, but are there to listen, share, have fun and improve everyone's evening. They are the ones who go home with a wallet full of valuable business cards.

DEIDRE, 34

❝ I attended a very glamorous business event recently and was warmly welcomed by a man there. He made a beeline for me as soon as I walked in, smiled, gave me a glass of champagne and asked me all about my work. It must have dawned on him slowly that I wasn't the Deirdre he thought I was – one that I suppose would be useful for his real estate business – and he began to look over my shoulder while I was talking, grunt replies rather than conversing, and at one point physically got up on his toes to see over the crowd for a more useful contact. It was his mistake. I may be a teacher, not a real estate guru, but my best friend is, and I advised her never to use this charmless man. ❞

Top five tips on how to spot a smarmy schmoozer!

1. They'll ask you a question and ignore your answer – they're too busy looking over your shoulder to see if someone more 'useful' has walked in.

2. They laugh a little too hard at your jokes and smile a bit too widely … without joy ever reaching their eyes.

3. Their first question is: 'What do you do?'

4. Their second question is: 'Who do you know?'

5. They cruise away from you to a new person, and go through exactly the same dialogue!

Natural networkers

The women in my life never cease to amaze me: be they my grandma who is still the most glamorous jetsetter despite illness and bereavement, or my mother who raised us alone while working to support her home and educating herself at the same time, or my deputy at work who overcame the sudden loss of a parent with class and a professionalism I will always admire.

Women have a lot of natural networking skills – which makes my job in this book much easier – but sometimes we just need to be reminded of them. Us girls are nurturers, protectors, friends, style icons, great brains and great beauties. The fact that most of us aren't showing off our characteristics is a great sign of our healthy attitudes. We don't need to throw on a power suit and down shots of whisky with the boys to prove we're as valuable in the workplace – or golf club – as they are!

We're also natural gossips – yes, we love to pass on news (beneficial to others), and we make fabulous listeners (good for us!). So as long as our gossip is generally positive, then it's a good thing. Don't let your boyfriend tell you off for over-the-garden-fence chit-chat.

Basic rules for lovely living

The world would be a much nicer place if people used common sense and good manners. The more you use these, the more people will like and trust you – and that's half your networking education done! Here are some golden rules that should never be forgotten:

◆ A smile will cost you nothing.

◆ Treat others how you would like to be treated yourself.

- Mind your Ps and Qs.

- A firm handshake is a must – weak wrist equals weak impression.

- If you can't say anything nice, don't say anything at all.

- Don't be rude to anyone on your way up ... in case you pass them again on your way down!

- Sorry seems to be the hardest word – but it shouldn't be.

- Queuing won't kill you.

The ultimate must-haves for achieving social acceptability

Before you make the most of your natural networking skills, or you train yourself up to become an excellent networker, look at the basic rules of pleasant living. You can never pay too much attention to the following:

- Being hygienic, clean and fragrant.

- Being neatly turned out: stain-, crease- and tear-free.

- Being polite, punctual and alert.

- Being generous, fair and understanding.

- Being the best you can be – whatever that is!

Always be on your best behaviour

Because you never know where your next boss, best friend or boyfriend is going to come from, you should always try to behave well – and by that I mean try not to do or say anything you wouldn't want other people to hear or know about. We all muck up, but if you can sleep soundly in your bed at night knowing you tried your best, you'll be all right. And good manners and kindness go a long way ... with the right kind of people!

Golden greetings

Networking isn't a difficult science. Sometimes its rules are as simple as greeting people correctly and bidding them farewell warmly. Yes, what goes on between the meet and greet and the au revoir is totally important ... but you can never put too high a price on the correct ciao!

Hello

Shouldn't saying hello be the simplest thing in the world? If done correctly, yes. And saying hello to someone for the first time is when you will make that all-important first impression. So, smile and hold eye contact (for longer than three seconds, but less than ten) while making your spoken greeting or shaking a hand. If you are in a different country, make the effort and use their language to say hi. If you're with others, introduce them, too, so that they can exchange greetings. If you're waiting to be introduced, don't turn your back, yawn or walk off. This is the height of rudeness and will not do you any favours.

Goodbye

Don't do overly emotional cheerios unless your beloved is off to sail the high seas for three months. A simple handshake or wave is a suitable au revoir for a new acquaintance or colleague. A quick hug or peck on the cheek will suffice for a friend. Please don't weep, drop to your knees and make them promise to see you again soon – or don't do the opposite. Never walk off mid-conversation, or leave the host of an event, without signing out correctly.

Kiss, kiss

One of the nightmares of modern society is who to kiss, when and how. The globe is shrinking with different cultures demanding a different 'pecking' order. If in doubt, put out your hand firmly in front of you, offering your palm for a quick shake. If your greeter pulls your forward for a kiss, at least by offering your right arm to his or her right arm, it will be clear which cheek you should go to first. If (cringe almighty!) the worst happens and you accidentally lip-lock, don't worry. We've all done it. Laugh it off, or ignore your misdemeanour if you sense your partner in crime would prefer it.

How many times should you kiss? I kiss friends and family once; colleagues, new acquaintances and luvvies get two; foreign dignitaries if they keep cheek swapping get three or four. Who's to stop them?

Sadly, when networking you will be forced to kiss more people than you wish to – but take comfort in the fact that this is not a full-on snog – in fact your lips should merely brush their cheek for a second. And never use tongues. Or hands.

NB Naughty words. Remember when networking, and in life in general, swearing can be considered offensive and terribly off-putting. Try to hold off on the cor blimeys until you know a person well and are assured they consider a few cheeky rude words funny or necessary rather than shocking. Never, ever swear in a job interview or when visiting future in-laws for the first time. And try to keep gesticulation to a minimum, too! You don't want to make the guest list for the top event in your industry, only to knock over the president's cocktail with your flamboyant gestures. Flipping the bird is never acceptable (unless you're a rather hard rapper who is purely reading this book as research for your next set of lyrics).

Does your accent affect your networking ability?

Although your accent shouldn't affect your networking ability, sadly, old-fashioned, misjudged stereotypes still pervade all societies! Of course, not all Americans are addicted to hamburgers, not all Italians are philanders and nor are all the Scots mean. Some people want to label the world ... but it doesn't work. And even if you have an accent that is considered lower class or ugly, you can change people's perceptions.

If you choose a field in which you want to succeed, I truly believe that energy, enthusiasm and talent will win over your upbringing or social class.

When I decided (aged ten) to become a journalist, no one else in my respectable, working-class London East End family had ever been to university and I certainly didn't know any other journalists, so nepotism wasn't an option for me. I got on the ladder with determination and self-belief and climbed it with hard work and good ideas. I didn't change my accent and I didn't hide my past, although I saw a few others around me trying to. Everything you experience, from your childhood to today, helps to make you who you are. Life is about learning lessons and lessons learned. If you're a good person, don't change – and certainly don't justify your past, your family, or your home.

'Different strokes for different folks' and all that – don't be embarrassed to be you!

If your accent is so strong that people can't understand you, and you're finding communication socially handicapping, perhaps you could have coaching in toning it down. I'm not talking about elocution lessons to put a plum in your mouth, just a speech therapist who can offer hints on slowing down and softening words to make you understandable.

Izzy, 24

❝ I moved to London from Paris two years ago but still I encounter prejudice and ignorance about my accent. Some men find it sexy – but sometimes assume things about romancing me that aren't true. And a bigger negative is that if I ever clash with a colleague (I have an important job, meeting clients for an advertising agency) and we disagree over something, it is too easy for them to say 'No one understands you!' or 'You're foreign, you don't get it!' It is very dismissive and upsetting. Actually, what I offer is a more international approach and a fresh agenda ... and the intelligent people I work with (including my bosses, thank God!) get that. ❞

How to remember people's names

Remembering others' names can be a nightmare, especially when you're being introduced to many people at the same time. The first trick is actually to *listen*! So often people are too busy smiling liking a goon or admiring the new acquaintance's Jimmy Choos that actually paying attention to what is being said is the last thing on their mind. Listen to the name and then repeat it. Yes, repeat it parrot-style immediately back at them. Now comes the time for a little mind trick: mentally try to link the name to something you will remember as soon as possible. Is it picturing a flower for a name like Rose, Hollie, Poppy, or something rather more sinister like your awful Great-Aunt Leslie who shares a name with your new friend? Use the name as much as you can straight away in the conversation; just saying it a few times will help it stick. And then, if at all possible, get their business card, or jot down their details in a diary.

JACQUI, 31

❛ At a very busy, bustling Christmas soirée last year, I misheard a name and spent the whole evening calling a lovely lady called Katie, Cacee. I even commented on what an unusual name she had – *and* introduced her to others. I don't think this was my networking faux pas though. I wish she had quietly corrected me ... before some drunken buffoon pointed out my mistake loudly in front of both of us as I was leaving. ❜

Other people forget, too!

If you're standing in a group and you haven't been introduced to the others by the host or mutual friend, go ahead and introduce yourself. Your poor intermediary is probably squirming with embarrassment at having forgotten one of your names or job titles. We've all been there.

Secrets of Success

◆ Networking is not just an excuse to pull. Of course, if you find love while networking that's great, but networking is about more that just sharking members of the opposite sex.

◆ Don't enter a new business group and flirt outrageously (or actually date) more than one person in it. It will make you seem fickle and floozie-ish.

◆ Networking is not about scrounging for freebies. You shouldn't just be nice to the woman who owns a villa in St Lucia because she has a villa in St Lucia ... don't you think the poor woman can see through these Scrooge-antics by now?

◆ Gossiping is a natural part of networking – finding out what's going on in other companies or with your managerial rival is important for you. But remember this golden rule of gossip: don't say anything you would be embarrassed to say to the person's face. Gossip does have a nasty way of getting back to the person being talked about – and normally in a twisted, dramatised state!

◆ If you're not brave enough to go up to a group and say hello, then smile instead – this will instantly warm strangers to you and it's easy.

◆ If there is someone at an event that you really want to meet, make a beeline for a mutual acquaintance if you have one, or introduce yourself to a less nerve-wracking colleague of your desired goal and hope for an introduction. Or, if you're forced to do the worst, follow her to the powder room and just happen to be between her and the paper towels. Remember that classic episode of *Sex and the City* when Carrie be-friended an infamously difficult maître d' by giving her a much-needed tampon? You could have such luck. This is only if it's someone of the same sex, obviously.

◆ Beware of your lipstick! Not only can it make you look like a bloody-toothed seventeenth-century wench if you get it on your teeth but it can also leave a mark when you greet some-one. If they're left working a room with a big painted smacker on their cheek they won't be happy later when they finally get to a mirror. If you do leave a SWALK, apologise, point it out and offer to dab it off. Don't go straight in with a damp tissue.

◆ You can't be loved by everybody, every time. Some people just won't 'get' you – but this has more to do with them and their insecurities than you if you know you have been polite, kind and fair. Lose them from your life. They're not worth you (as a nice person) worrying or stressing about.

◆ Don't just see networking as a short-term charm offensive to get that pay rise or job offer. Networking can be incorporated into your everyday life, from when you're an enthusiastic trainee to a stay-at-home mum. Networking is the art of building alliances, making friends and making your life – and the lives of everyone else around you – that little bit easier.

Chapter Two

Body beautiful

F ONLY NETWORKING WERE as simple as just saying the right things. Not only has everyone become more interested in fashion and what your clothes say about you but also people seem to have become more educated about what your body language is saying about you and how it expresses what you feel about everyone else. These days you need more than a wonderful wardrobe to make a good impression. A lesson in top moves and grooves is totally essential for any wannabe networking genius.

Dress for success

A picture paints a thousand words – so make sure you look a pretty picture. A first impression is formed mostly on what you look like – what you say has very little to do with it. Research has shown that people form their opinion of you in the first three seconds – and that includes taking in and judging your clothes, hairstyle, jewellery, and so on. This is important to know when choosing what to wear to an interview or to your first day in a new office. And remember: the better dressed you are the better you will feel. That's why I always wear special, matching underwear on important occasions – no one is going to see it, but I know I'm wearing it and it makes me feel groomed and confident.

Top ten tips for fashion fabulousness

At work, in meetings and in interviews you must pay attention to your overall appearance – dress to kill the competition:

1. For an interview, dress up – look as if you've got the job already and you're marching the corridors with confidence.

2. Clothing shouldn't detract from your persona; it should just subtly add to the good impression your persona creates.

3. When in an office, even if the dress code is casual, smarten up. It shows you're making an effort and want to do well.

4. Dress for the job you want – not the job you have. Simulate your seniors' style.

5. You're professional. Don't dress tarty. Legs or cleavage – never both.

6. You can dress like a crazy punk with your mates, but at work or when at important social events your aim shouldn't be to stand out. It should be to look elegant, smart and together. Don't try on a new teenage fashion trend for the work Christmas party.

7. For an important interview or meeting, choose an outfit you've worn before and feel comfortable in. Try on the outfit a few days before to make sure it still fits and doesn't need dry-cleaning or repairing. Check for missing buttons, scuffs or frayed edges.

8. Pick your colours carefully. Blue conveys trust, confidence and control. Red conveys competition, anger and

sex. Any colour can work if balanced with others, but never use top to toe in one shade, other than black (and even that is more flattering broken up with jewellery or different-coloured accessories).

9. Carry all your personal items in a bag; bulging pockets and a sagging coat lining ruin the cut of even the best suit or jacket – and don't do much for your figure either.

10. Pay attention to invitations. Look for the dress code instructions. Research your new place of work to find out what dress code is expected and accepted.

SPECIAL TOUCHES

- Keep jewellery classy, and real if possible. No Christmas-decoration earrings, animal-inspired necklaces or tiaras before 8.00 p.m. please.

- Always check your appearance – front and back – in a mirror before you leave the house.

- Shoes should be polished, unscuffed and comfortable. You might look a million dollars but if you're limping with blisters, you'll seem like a tramp.

- There's no point being groomed if the handbag you're clutching is battered and stuffed to the brim with rubbish. Invest in a good, subtle bag and fill it with only the necessities: phone, purse, keys, make-up bag, and so on.

- At the end of each season, dry-clean and store your seasonal clothes carefully. It's one less thing for a busy lady like you to worry about.

- Be subtle with your scent – you don't want to kill plants and small animals when you walk into a room.

- Use make-up sparingly – and check you're not rubbing off foundation on your collar or getting lipstick on your teeth.

- Keep a spare pair of tights in your desk at work and in your handbag for emergencies and if you're prone to holes and ladders.

- Motto T-shirts can be cool/hilarious … or a bit sad. I've got a gold one that says 'B is for Bling', which I've got my doubts about but continue to wear. But not to the office and certainly not to an important meeting or event.

- Natural fabrics rock – wool, silk and cotton look smart and expensive.

What not to wear

When planning an all-over 'look', avoid fluorescent fabrics, animal-print leggings, the bra-less approach, loud patterns, blue eye liner, bubble perms, cowboy hats, the gelled-up-fringe do, and dungarees – and keep the following to the beach: sarongs, baseball caps, bikini tops as outer wear (no, Victoria Beckham, no!), see-through dresses and kaftans.

How to dress for other networking events

Out of a professional environment, you can spice things up a bit – just remember what suits your size… and the event.

Weddings

Everyone knows you meet a variety of interesting strangers at other people's weddings. And the good thing is they are forced to talk to you – there's no escape! Obviously, it's not appropriate to wear dark and sober suits to a wedding – the office dress code goes out the window. But it is still important to dress with dignity and for your shape. Stick to colours that suit you – even girly pinks and pretty pastels are fine at weddings. Know – and admit – your size. Squeezing your bottom into too-small trousers is not big or clever – but it will make your bottom look big. Basically, the perfect wedding guest looks well groomed and as though she's made an effort, without upstaging the bride, the bride's mother, and without flashing too much flesh at the vicar!

Dates

More on date networking in Chapter 10, but when dressing for a man remember: (a) You want him to respect you in the morning; (b) He doesn't want to date his mother or his niece, so dress your age; and (c) You want to feel beautiful and confident.

Don't show cleavage and legs – it's one or the other; and don't wear anything too noisy, such as jangly bracelets – they will distract the man from your enlightening conversation.

Family functions

You never know when a distant auntie or long-lost cousin will embrace your business plan and lend you cash, or come up with a fun idea to help your new hobby. Don't put them off you by wearing offensive T-shirts with political statements or swear words printed across the front. And try to look like you've matured from that slovenly teenager they knew ten years ago – dress up and sharpen up.

Working out

So many of us meet interesting and inspiring people at the gym these days. Sadly for many of us, it's the only place that we feel we have to visit on a regular basis – more than even visiting our dear old grandma. Stay cool when you're working up a sweat by dressing appropriately for your club: make sure your shorts aren't so short the exercise class can see what you had for breakfast when you do a leg stretch. And do use deodorant – the person on the treadmill next to you isn't going to be chummy if you're humming! If you're using the swimming pool, make sure the fabric of your costume doesn't go see-through when you get wet.

Night-time networking

If you get an invite to a function in the evening and the dress code is stated, always stick to it. Don't customise or ignore instructions. You'll feel like Dolly Parton or Waynetta Slob, depending on which side of the dress-up/dress-down scale you fall! If there are no instructions, for casual evening elegance stick to simple shapes that suit you: a trouser suit with interesting jewellery, or a well-fitting dress with a cashmere cardigan to keep off the chills. Accessorise with care – the right shoes say a lot about a girl – and keep labels understated.

What is body language?

Body language is the way you consciously, or most often subconsciously, display your feelings and emotions to the world. You know, how celebrity magazines and newspaper supplements love to focus in on an actor's frozen smile or a royal handshake and then psychoanalyse what they were *really* thinking. Of course, once these strangely ill-fitting moves are pointed out to us, the readers, we see immediately: the star hates his wife, the Duke thinks his new acquaintance is common, and so on.

But even without the help of a psychoanalyst, we know who makes us feel comfortable (someone who smiles warmly and has a firm handshake) and who doesn't (someone who stares at us for a full 20 seconds after being introduced).

Some people are naturally socially awkward – maybe they grew up in a different culture from the one they mix in now, or perhaps as children they were never taken to restaurants or parties and find the whole thing intimidating.

We all have different past stories, but a few hints and tips (as simple as how to stand while having a conversation) will allow you to feel more comfortable, and for the people you are networking with to feel relaxed and at ease in your presence.

Don't stand so close to me!

Sting and those boys from the Police had a point. The distance you stand when meeting someone, or when just holding a conversation, could have you pinned down as a pervert or a socially stand-offish weirdo.

◆ Too close is 0–30cm (0–12in). If you can see blackheads on noses or smell bad breath, move away! Being this close to someone who isn't your lover, mother or brother will make you seem overly familiar, needy and perhaps a little sexually suggestive.

◆ The perfect distance is between 30cm and 1m (12in and 3ft 3in). You can hear, you can physically interact if necessary (that is, a jokey tap on the arm) but you're not grinning down on the other person with intent.

Embarrassing things our body does to us, and how to cope

We can say the right thing, wear the right thing, but sometimes shit happens. If you tread on someone's foot, apologise. Hey, even if they tread on yours, apologise. Your foot must have been in the way. Saying sorry over small stuff like that just makes life easier. The same goes for barging into someone on the street. I was marching through Times Square the other day, when an equally busy, speedy woman was hurtling towards me. We clashed. I said, 'Oops, sorry!' She said, 'Stupid, rabid F**K!' And she looked so nice, in her smart suit and heels. I was a little offended at first, especially as her elbow had caught my ribcage and it hurt … but I thought that such a public overreaction about a mutual mistake says more about her than me. And rather than worrying that I, in fact, was a 'stupid, rabid F**K', I was pretty sure that she must be. When encountering silly, pointless aggression on the streets like that, ignore it and don't let it wind you up or upset your day. If they continue, run away – it's not cowardice. It's called being sensible.

Other embarrassing things your body can do to you – in fact the most embarrassing things in the whole world (skirt tucked in knickers excepted) are to burp, or, particularly, to fart in public. I farted once in a very stuffy, posh London City office, in front of my two very grand and respectable bosses. Time stood still for what seemed like an eternity. My cheeks (both sets probably) burned bright red and my eyes fleeted to the exit longingly. Because they were gentlemen, one of them coughed, the other changed the subject and no mention was ever made of my misdemeanour. This is the correct action all round. And their politeness was returned when, the following month, while sharing a London taxi to a meeting, the taxi braked suddenly at some traffic lights and one of them was flung into the other's lap – face down – and we all managed to continue discussing Thatcher's reign without a stop for breath or a suppressed giggle.

If you do break wind or burp, and something has to be said, just apologise (if you own up, it's not such a big deal) and move on. Even Madonna burps. Allegedly.

Falling over in public is a nightmare. As a kid, I fell over five times a day and didn't notice. Now, if I fall over I'm in shock for the rest of the day and bruised for a week. I suppose it's different tripping over when you are 180cm (5ft 11in) from when you were 92cm (3ft)!

If you're not bleeding or broken, get up as quickly as possible before a crowd of concerned strangers gather. If you can manage a laugh and a 'silly me' thrown in for good measure, all the better. It's worth keeping a spare pair of tights in the office or in your handbag in case of emergencies like this. If you have really hurt yourself, stay on the ground (this is if you have not tripped up in the middle of the road, of course), take advantage of the caring passers-by and don't mind crying. It'll stop anyone laughing.

Body language you can control

Now that the basics and embarrassing bodily bits are out of the way, we can discuss the simplest ways to give a good impression without opening your mouth or handing over large sums of cash!

Making an entrance

Putting one foot in front of another and walking into a room full of strangers is difficult if you're shy or feeling a little under par ... but a famous movie star (sorry, can't remember which one) once said you should walk into any room imagining a rainbow over your head. It will make you happy and charismatic. It does work. A psychic actress I met once in Los Angeles (I know, I know) once told me she could see a star above my head, and that it was beautiful and powerful. If I ever have to do a speech in front of hundreds of people, or I'm forced to discipline someone in the office, I remember this and my confidence comes flooding back. So there's a lesson for you all: go to Tinseltown and find a white witch! (Bizarrely, I have just watched a TV show with successful British export, comic Tracey Ullman, where she states she was told from a young age that she had a star above her head and it drove her on to take America by storm.)

THE EYES HAVE IT

- When you say hello, maintain eye contact for three seconds, then look away – any longer and you'll look confrontational or a bit spaced out. But continue to look someone in the eye throughout your chit-chat. Avoiding someone's gaze raises alarm bells of shiftiness or lying.

- No extreme blinking please, but do remember to blink sometimes.

- Don't look out into the distance during a conversation (you'll look spaced out) or up to the side (you'll look as if you're being dishonest).

- Make eye contact regularly and frequently throughout a conversation – don't let your eyes wander to the handsome waiter over your chat-chum's shoulder.

- Don't do funny tricks like going cross-eyed or flipping your eyelids back. It's gross ... and the wind really might change!

- If you can't get used to contact lenses, who cares. Rather than having red-raw, weepy eyes, treat yourself to a fashionable pair of glasses and remember that the people who called you four-eyes at school were unimaginative and stupid.

A smile costs nothing

There is no better way to greet an old friend or new acquaintance than with a full-on Cheshire-cat grin – if it's genuine. People can pick out fakes, and an insincere grin is easily spotted, and detestable!

There are three golden rules to meeting new people: smile, don't moan and don't cross your arms. Really. For God's sake, smile!

When walking into a room full of strangers, don't rush. Take a few deep breaths, think happy (a natural smile will follow) and scan the room with your head held high. Catch the eye of someone else smiley and on their own, and calmly make your way over to start a conversation. Don't run.

What a poser!

I used to laugh at those silly bimbos who would pout and preen the minute they saw they were going to have their picture taken. But in my job, not only do I attend lots of shoots where I see photographers, models and celebrities working together to get the best result, but I've also been caught out gurning and grimacing on a red carpet once too often. So I actually asked, how should you stand when you're having your photo taken (or trying to look seductive from a distance if you've got your eye on a fellow across the bar)?

Well, here's how:

- When having an important photo taken, ask the snapper to count you in so you know not to blink or move suddenly. Half-shut eyelids turn a perfectly sober networker into a schmoozing lush.

- Study your face in the mirror and look at old photos – everyone (unless you're Kate Moss or Liz Hurley) has a good side and a bad side, normally to do with the size and shape of facial features. Find out what yours is – and when posing, turn that side of your face to the camera. It's more flattering, as you will be showing your best side and not looking at the camera head on. Since I learned this trick a couple of years ago, everyone has commented that I am photogenic. I have a square head which can look bulky in photos – turning side on reduces the effect! Hoorah!

- For an extra shine, lick your lips and your teeth just before a photo is taken.

- If it's a particularly important portrait, don't worry about looking vain – quickly brush your hair and reapply your lip gloss.

- For an instant slim-down, suck your tummy in, tuck your bottom under and push your breasts forwards in a perky manner. Stand sideways and turn your top half towards the lens, one leg placed in front of the other. Placing your hands on your hips will slim your arms.

◆ Don't look miserable in photos – even if you are. Try and recall something funny to add a little spark to your eyes.

◆ If you're posing in a group, be careful not to stand next to someone in the same colour as you (you'll disappear) or in a clashing colour to you (you'll make people dizzy).

◆ Oh, it seemed so funny at the time to make a 'V' sign behind that poor man's head, or to pretend to be a muscleman in that picture. For a long time, I had a ridiculous tendency to stick my tongue out in photos. Just remember: it's fun to be the court jester, but not to capture it in photographs that could well last longer than you! Especially at your company's conference.

◆ And as a last resort (this is very cheeky but ...) most people shoot on digital these days, so if you know you were moving or had your eyes closed, kindly ask the man behind the shutter to delete it and take another. It's easy with digital.

Hand job

Shaking hands is easy, but people get it wrong so often. Remember: be firm, not vice-like, and while shaking, lean in slightly. It makes the gesture warmer and you will be remembered for it. A little squeeze of their right elbow with your left hand as you shake hands will also make a good impression. Tickling their palm as you touch will not.

Don't try and do any fancy down-with-the-kids hand gestures. They're embarrassing in anyone over 16.

CLAIRE, 33

❝ At my boss's leaving do, I decided to present her with a bouquet, just from me – to thank her for all the advice she'd given me over the years. Despite working together for a long time, we weren't outside buddies and were still formal with each other. I'd never kissed her in my life. Anyway, I handed her the bouquet and thought now would be the time to give her a peck on the cheek. She still thought we were just on shaking-hands terms I think, because as I moved in she thrust out her hand and accidentally grabbed my boob. The whole office saw and I was scarlet for a week. She was lucky – she left! ❞

Secrets of Success

◆ Simple style says expensive style.

◆ No pain, no gain – and beauty *is* pain. Get waxed, exfoliated, extractions ... the pain lasts a second, the effect lasts a month.

◆ Carry an umbrella. The drowned-rat look is not good.

◆ A light tan equals healthy; a burned face equals lobster. Wear sun-tan lotion with a high SPF (sun-protection factor).

◆ A flash of a dimpled thigh or saggy cleavage can turn even the strongest stomach. Decorum when dressing, ladies, decorum!

◆ Don't suffer embarrassing bodily functions in silence. Excessive flatulence, sweating, belching or bad breath are all signs of a deeper health issue. Go and talk to your doctor. And in the meantime, cope with dignity; pack an emergency kit for your handbag and office (breath mints, facial tissues, indigestion tablets, and so on).

◆ Before greeting people with your megawatt smile, check there's no spinach in between your teeth. Make it the last thing on your checklist when you've glanced at your hair and make-up.

◆ When meeting people in social or professional situations the important thing to remember is to slow down. When you get nervous everything speeds up – your heart rate, your breathing, your speech, and your movements. Take a breath and slow down. It will make you appear calm, cool and fabulous.

◆ When you're at a party, limit the chances of finding yourself slumped on the floor by not drinking too much. Alcohol doesn't calm your nerves. It will make you seem crazy and will cloud your judgement, making you think that grabbing your boss's arse is acceptable, a friendly gesture in fact.

◆ Spend money where it matters – on a good haircut, a good suit, fine-quality shoes – people will notice these things about you. And simply knowing you have them will boost your confidence.

◆ Hey, if you're mortified about something to do with your personal appearance – sort it out. Every day you spend worrying about it is a day wasted. Start that diet, save up for your teeth whitening and go to the doctor about your acne.

◆ The easiest way to show someone you are interested in what they are saying is to mimic their body language and actions. Don't go all Simon Says, but reflect their position – they will subconsciously appreciate your encouragement and feel comfortable with you; but be careful, too much mutual hair flicking and it could look like a come-on!

◆ The best things in life are free – and a smile comes cheap! Also, it has been medically proven that giving a grin improves your health. So do it.

Chapter Three

How to be your own best friend

IFE IS HARD. HOLDING DOWN a job and earning a good wage makes it even harder. But there are skills you can learn to make your working life easier as well as making you happy, respected and confident in all areas. What's the point of earning a lot of money if you're despised, or you never get to see your family? This chapter is about being the best you can be, while keeping your eye on what is important.

Confidence boosters

Even the most beautiful, charming, intelligent women in the world have a crisis of confidence at times – and if they say they don't they're lying or too vain to be admired. However, there are some easy things to remember to make that life-challenging, knee-trembling, pathetic feeling go away.

Personal confidence boosters

◆ Think about a time when you felt truly happy and secure; imagine how you felt and remind yourself how great it was – and that you can feel that way again.

◆ Write down five things you know you're good at and stick them onto your fridge, or by the front door so that you see them every time you go out.

◆ Ask your family to email you, saying why they love you.

◆ Think about your favourite celebrity. Now think about what you have in common … and what you actually have better!

♦ Wear matching underwear. Knowing you are wearing great things under your clothes will make you feel special.

♦ Pick a fragrance that you love and others love on you, then spritz yourself with the scent every time you go out.

♦ Spend some time and money on yourself. Go shopping, visit a spa, take a holiday.

♦ Take up an evening class. Learning a new skill means not only will you get practice at meeting new people but you'll also have something new to talk about.

♦ Have a make-up lesson, and visit a clothes colour specialist. You'll find out exactly what suits you.

♦ A great haircut makes every woman feel fantastic – peruse the latest styles then get a classic, stylish cut and colour that's easy to maintain.

♦ Get fit. You don't have to join an expensive gym to get those good hormones racing round your body; go swimming, walking, cycling, dancing – you'll notice a fab physical and mental improvement.

Public confidence boosters

♦ Don't let someone misinterpret your shyness or lack of social confidence as rudeness or indifference. Explain that you're shy upfront. Most people will then make an effort with you.

♦ Make sure you wear an outfit you feel comfortable in (and know you look good in) when you're going out to an interview, meeting or social event.

◆ Focus on someone or something when you walk into a crowded room. Don't let your eyes dart about nervously; you'll get dizzy and look peculiar.

◆ Don't worry if you blush – it looks charming and hot cheeks will make people warm to you.

◆ Work on your posture. Stand tall for an instant boost (and to lose a few unwanted pounds).

◆ The old rules are the best – if you walk into a room and feel a bit intimidated, imagine everyone is naked. They won't seem so scary without their pants on.

◆ Don't drink heavily. It won't sedate your nerves; it will make you paranoid or make you embarrass yourself. Neither is good.

◆ Smile, even when you don't feel like it!

NATASHA, 38

❛ I always fast-forward ten minutes when I'm nervous. I don't concentrate on why I'm scared or anxious; I focus on the treat I will give myself once it's over. Last month, my company flew me out to Los Angeles where I had to give a speech in front of 400 people – including my boss. Everyone else was drinking and dancing, I couldn't as I wanted to stay sober and cool, so I said to myself when my time in the spotlight arrived, "Two minutes, then I'm going to have a glass of champagne and make a request to the DJ." It worked, thinking of that, I went on stage with a smile and an end in sight! ❜

Alternative therapies – or hocus-pocus?

A lot of people who are chronically shy or agoraphobic turn to the alternative side, such as hypnotherapy, for help when looking to boost their confidence – and it works. Is the cure psychosomatic; is it all in the mind? Who cares, if it works? The mind is a powerful thing. Contact your doctor about the nearest practitioner. Acupuncture also helps with stress and its side effects. I'm a huge advocate of it – I had hourly sessions for a year and whether it was mind over matter or not, those needles worked wonders!

Confidence tricks

We all have moments of insecurity. People assume I'm very confident because of my job (and the fact I'm nearly 1.8m (6ft) tall makes me appear stronger than I am, too), but sometimes I have bad days when I don't want to leave my office or go to sit with nine strangers at a charity dinner. How do I get through it? Sorry to be so very British, but sometimes it's a case of putting up and shutting up, and a stiff upper lip. We all have to do things we'd rather not, but the quicker we stop complaining and get on with it, the quicker it's over. When heading into a hideous meeting – normally in a room full of men at least ten years older than me – I literally take a deep breath, think how I'll look back on this in a few years' time and be proud of myself ... and imagine them all naked. Yes, it works. Or I imagine them to be failed superheroes (along the lines of *The Incredibles*), and that under their grey suits are more interesting one-piece outfits.

If all else fails, I remember that it's just a job and everyone makes mistakes. If I say something stupid in a meeting, I might remember it and squirm and cringe all afternoon but others won't.

Don't forget: everyone is more focused on themselves and how they are perceived. They are not scrutinising you quite so closely.

Above all else, you must know that you are in this position because you are the best for it. Your company trusts you to make a good impression, to talk eloquently and to be a great ambassador for it. This shouldn't be an added pressure; it should be a boost. Out of all the modern girls out there, they have chosen you!

How to sing your own praises ... without turning everyone deaf!

There is a fine line between telling the truth and being a total bighead – and no one likes a bighead! I've got a friend who sniggers at everyone else's achievements, while expecting us to listen wide-eyed as she recounts another exaggerated tale of her success with the clarinet/scales/new man at work. People are more likely to offer praise – and believe you – if you:

- ◆ Don't shout about everything you've done, just the key things.

- ◆ Listen and congratulate them on their news, too.

- ◆ Wait for someone else to bring up your good news for you.

- ◆ Accept compliments with honesty and humbleness.

- ◆ Tell it how it is. Don't dramatise.

Self-promotion

While keeping grounded and humble, you do need to perfect the 'hard self-sell' when networking for a new job, promotion or an important position in an organisation. The hard sell always comes better from someone else, so talk to a trusted senior colleague or friend who knows the right people, and ask them to spread the word on your qualities and merits. It won't sound arrogant at all if coming from someone else.

If you are left to do your own selling, think of ways to lead the conversation into an area beneficial to you. If talking about holidays, say you always go to France because you speak fluent French. Turn things that could be considered boastful into funny tales; for example, 'I can sing and dance a bit, so my mum was very proud that I got the lead in the university play – until she had to sit through me battling on stage like a croaky frog because of my glandular fever. Bless her; her moment to be proud was stolen by my swollen glands!' This plays down your performing skills, while highlighting that you are a trooper and won't let people down – and shows you have a caring side. That's the thing to do; tell stories that show you failing comfortably or with good spirit, without really highlighting any serious flaws.

Personal problems

No matter how many self-help mantras you say, if you make the following very basic faux pas while networking you will notice people switching off and disliking you:

◆ **Being pompous.** You don't know it all – no one does. While circulating and chatting, listen to what others are saying. Respect their opinion even if it is not your own. People can help you by offering their opinions and advice.

◆ **Being a wallflower.** Powerful people meet – and remember – other powerful people. You need to make yourself stand out, for good reasons. Don't go mad, but do assert yourself when out in public. Be confident enough to pay others compliments and to tell a few jokes.

◆ **Being clueless is an utter no-no.** I've got a friend who proudly announces when a chat about a celebrity or trend comes up, 'I don't watch television and I certainly don't read magazines!' Her snootiness backfires – she looks out of the loop and can't join in general chit-chat that her peer group enjoys. Read a newspaper every day – it helps.

◆ **Being a social stalker is not good.** Monopolising someone's time at an event, following them to the bathroom and knocking on the cubicle door, glowing with pride when they ask you to hold their drink … creepy. However much in awe you are of someone, don't act like a mad Tom Jones groupie and throw your knickers at them. Show respect by listening to them, asking for advice and showing good manners.

◆ **Being a liar is never good** – and when you are relying on others' goodwill and contacts to help you out, as you often are when networking, it's a disaster. You'll get found out, pure and simple, and then who will invite you for an interview or to join their committee? No one.

NB Remember, too, that people don't like to discuss (and will remember you as being the idiot who brought it up) their medical history, their political views, their mortgage, their salary, their age, their weight or their partner's gynaecological bits. Stay shtum.

Staying true to yourself

When you're desperately trying to get ahead, pushing for that promotion or praying for that dream of a new company to take off, it's easy to become stressed and lose sense of reality. Your reality. If you're out every night networking and on your best behaviour, you can become consumed with work, money and climbing the corporate ladder. These things are important, of course, but so are family, friends, you-time, your health and your mental state. I worked so hard last year, launching a magazine in a new country, that I made myself ill. It wasn't the long hours, the decision making, or the external challenges that brought me down. It was the inner-office politics and the nastiness of some of my colleagues. I handled it thanks to my loved ones, and treated the negative people forced into my life as pantomime villains – it's hard to let people who are theatrically duplicitous and jealous stress you out. As long as you know you're being decent, fair and kind, let the losers scrabble among themselves.

◆ **Even when work seems like the most important thing in the world,** take ten minutes a day to keep in touch with those who will be there for you in the long run. Your grandma would love to hear from you! When you're on holiday, take ten minutes to send everyone a postcard. Read a funny newspaper article; send the link to all your girlfriends. Use your time wisely – chat to your mum on your five-minute walk from the office to your bus stop. Keep a diary with everyone's birthdays in it so you never forget, and stock up on cards, wrapping paper and universal trinkets to stick in the post in case you're too busy to go out specifically. Also, remember that however tough your life is, someone will have it tougher. Take time out to go to see your university friend's new baby, or to go to your great-aunt's funeral, or to visit your dad's best friend in hospital.

♦ **Have a hobby** – something you really love. I love taking photographs, and I took a course that enabled me, for three hours a week, to return to being a pupil and forget all about the world outside. Even now, I can disappear with my camera and de-stress in an instant. Other friends have found the following to be relaxing and life-enhancing: reading groups, Bikram yoga, writing circles, swimming, joining a football or netball team, taking art classes, and joining a embroidery group.

♦ **Read.** Read newspapers, magazines, books. Read books that make you escape and chill out, and read books about your life stage or work dreams.

♦ **Spend time alone.** It's so tempting to rush through hours, days, weeks, years – yes, there is always something you should be doing: the laundry, the shopping, cleaning … But what matters more than these things is your well-being and mental health, and sometimes pushing yourself and setting too many deadlines is a bad thing. Take a long, hot bath with delicious bath oils; make the time to light the room with candles and dig out your favourite

CD to play. Take yourself off to bed on a Sunday afternoon with a hot chocolate and the paper for a snooze. Book yourself a pedicure at your favourite spa and prepare yourself a relaxing playlist on your iPod to take along with you. These small, selfish things can be the difference between a happy you and a frazzled you.

◆ **Look after your health.** Go to the gym. If you can't go to the gym, try to walk for at least half an hour a day. Don't take the lift; use the stairs. Think before you eat – yes, yes, keep the chocolate and the pizza but get enough green stuff, too. And get a check-up, have a blood test. Find out if taking any vitamins and minerals would help you.

◆ **Reminisce.** You're trying hard to be this successful career woman, but are you still 'you'? Think back to what you liked doing as a child, laugh with your siblings about old adventures, revisit teenage holiday sites, and organise a university reunion. What was important to you then is probably still important to you now – you may have just forgotten it. Dig a little deeper, dig out those old photo albums, and dig up those dreams …

Beating emotional burnout

Modern Life is Rubbish, is the name of my favourite Blur album – and blimey, it's true! We work hard to survive, to get onto the property ladder, to afford the expensive gym membership that allows us to conform to society's idea of the perfect woman, to find ourselves a date in this ever more cynical society of men, who aren't ready to settle down (or be tied down) yet, and to have babies. And we need to keep our jobs if we do!

It's exhausting, but 'nobody said it was easy', sang Coldplay. When you're at the end of your tether, worried you're about to lose control of your temper or your mind, regroup with these top ten tips:

1. **Cry.** Having a good old weep feels self-indulgent but it is the body's way of releasing harmful toxins and shedding painful emotions. Keeping them in is much more damaging.

2. **See the funny side of life.** When I was getting stressed out by the aforementioned nasty colleague, I thought of a funny thing to focus on. He always wore his trousers too high, over his huge tummy. I would ignore his insults by imagining them getting higher and higher until all you could see was his balding head and glasses, peeking from the top. This enabled me to laugh at an otherwise difficult time.

3. **Chill out.** Try some self-relaxation techniques if you can't afford a massage. Breathe slowly and close your eyes. Imagine you are in a place where you feel happy and warm – be it in bed, on a beach, in your parents' back garden. Then tighten and slowly release your muscles, from the bottom (your toes) up to the top (your forehead). Continue to breathe deeply and slowly, then open your eyes and stay still for a few minutes, before getting on with your day.

4. **Talk to your good friends.** Ask them how they cope, what advice they can share, or at the very least, get them to take your mind off your own worries with a trip to the cinema or a night in with a bottle of Pinot Grigio.

5. **Say what you mean.** Trying to fit in all the time is tiring. Don't be offensive, but say what you mean and get stuff

off your chest. Find your voice and stick up for yourself. Be you and people will love it.

6. **When the office is draining you, get out.** Go for a ten-minute walk – even if it's just to get a coffee from around the block. A brisk walk boosts your mood, gets the endorphins moving and releases tension.

7. **Let down your barriers.** We all need to be strong in the boardroom and with our bosses, but sometimes we need to let it all go. Dismantle your barricades at home with your loved ones. This is a self-preservation society, and being strong is a skill, but sometimes we need to show what's in our heart and mind to be truly emotionally unburdened.

8. **Scream!** But not in the office. Find an isolated spot where you can let rip, like in the shower or in the car. Letting off steam in private is a great way of getting rid of anger and negative feelings. You'll feel ridiculous at first (I did!) but it works. I know a great, modern family who scream together before dinner every night and they're all remarkably well balanced!

9. **Colour yourself beautiful.** Choose one colour for your happy feelings (say, pink), and one for your sad (say, grey). Close your eyes. Imagine yourself pushing away negative grey clouds, and surrounding yourself with positive pink clouds. Imagine emerging through a black fog into a blue sky. Breathe out red, breathe in lavender. Colour therapy works.

10. **Listen to yourself.** Listen to your body. Be your own counsellor. Have an early night when you need one, avoid alcohol if you're down; indulge in a super-large box of chocolates if you fancy it. If you can feel

yourself getting easily irritated or stressed, lighten your mood by planning something positive – like a holiday or an Indian takeaway – even if it's only, for now, in your head!

NELL, 21

❝ I knew I was tired and unhappy, and that my sex drive was at an all-time low, and I knew it was because of work. But, of course, I thought complaining was a weakness so I battled on, fighting these feelings with boozy nights out, takeaways and rushed weekends away. I had a medical and my blood tests came back showing my white blood cell count was way too high – a sign that my body was fighting an attack, through stress or infection. It really made me think 'is it all worth it?' I instantly changed my approach. I realised that I came first, because without me my company had nothing. I started Pilates, taking vitamins, and forgot those panicked am-I-going-to-miss-the-plane weekend escapes, and planned a two-week turn-off-the-BlackBerry retreat in the sun instead. ❞

Secrets of Success

◆ The best advice I've ever been given is, 'Like yourself, trust yourself, follow your heart.' It works. Try it.

◆ Need a confidence boost? Don't be shy – tell your friends you're feeling down and need some inspiration. Ask them to email you a list of good things about yourself and why they love you as a friend.

◆ She who dares wins. Do it. Weigh up the pros, but don't take too long worrying about the cons. Trust your instincts and just do it. It's easier than you think.

◆ If you can feel yourself getting too stressed, talk to your GP or call a helpline. Don't suffer alone and don't feel embarrassed. Modern society has increased mental problems, but there are therapies and drugs that can help.

◆ Your glass is half full, not half empty. Always strive to be happy – even if it means following a difficult path for a time to get you there. Some decisions are hard to make, but let the combination of your heart and head lead you to a place where your future will be brighter.

◆ Make your own decisions. Ask others for advice and help, but, ultimately, don't let others dictate to you. Your choices will be your problems alone at night, so let them be your successes, too.

◆ Is it the placebo effect? Who cares! Take vitamins related to your worries. An all-purpose multivitamin is always good. And speak to a pharmacist or a doctor about the following pills. If you're stressed or unable to sleep, take 300mg of magnesium a day. If you're exhausted, ask your doctor about taking chromium. For depression, try avoiding alcohol and taking 5-HTP (5-hydroxytryptophan) instead. If you're feeling forgetful and not as sparkling as usual, try a vitamin B complex — such as B12 and folic acid, which have been proved to boost your memory. Check the correct quantity to take carefully.

Chapter Four

The good networker's tool kit

Now you've got the basics – you have fabulous manners, you look gorgeous and you have your worries and insecurities under control – you're ready to get equipped with the modern girl's totally can't-live-without networker's tool kit. Everything you need will be in your mentally stocked Hermes bag of communication and planning.

Ten ten rules for networking know-how

To become a networking supremo, you need to be efficient, diligent... and determined to succeed.

1 Contacts, contacts, contacts

Think of everyone you've ever met. Now shorten the list to people you respected, liked, looked up to, admired and got on well with. These are the people who could be handy to you. I'm not just talking about your university lecturers or your first boss, or even your dad's friends. Very often, people in unrelated fields have contacts they would be happy to share with you: a sister in New York who knows a great visa lawyer, or a neighbour who has just completed the course you want to know more about, for example. Cast your networking net as wide as you can and you'll be surprised by what you catch! Try your family friends, your doctor, your dentist, your university alumni, your hair-dresser, local politicians or journalists, ex-colleagues and former employees.

> **NB You will get warning bells about people** ... and
> sometimes you need to listen to these and trust your
> instincts. Only people that like and respect you will help you
> out in your quest for a business contact or a better job —
> don't waste time with troublemakers, liars, or the funda-
> mentally bitter and resentful types — why would they help
> you if they can't help themselves?

2 Network in your sleep

Well, not literally, but do remember that networking has no
boundaries and you never know when that great opportunity is going to come and bite you on the arse. You should
be alert and ready to dig for information anywhere and
everywhere. There are the obvious places — everywhere
from class reunions and cocktail parties to education classes
— where it would be disappointing to leave without a few
business cards shoved in your pocket. Good networkers,
however, aren't surprised when a future boss warms up on
the treadmill next to them at the gym. Good networkers are
flexible and can see beyond conference-room walls and job
interviews. How you handle a random exchange can turn a
chance meeting with an affable high-flyer into a pivotal
moment in your career. And even if that person on the sunlounger next to the jacuzzi has nothing obvious to offer
you, they may have something you can pass on to a friend
or contact. It's not always just about you!

3 Be a good Girl Guide

Be prepared. I don't want to get serious about this but networking can be tough, almost political, stuff. You need to

prepare yourself as someone going into a self-improvement battle. It's essential that you are well turned out and armed with good manners, but you do need a few extra weapons, too. Think about what you are trying to achieve by networking, and what information you need to have stored in your head to make these achievements.

It may sound strange, but get to know yourself – plan a one-minute presentation in your head so that if called upon you could (in an entertaining way) list your skills, talents and accomplishments. And do your homework. You might look the bee's knees, but if you sashay into a room with little knowledge of who is in there and why, suddenly you won't look so good. Find out who will be at an event, and plan your introduction and key questions. Think about what you want to have got out of each meeting at the end of it, who are the key players at each event, and what you want to find out from them. Do remember, however, as much as you'd love to plan every single exchange, you can't control everything and you have to be flexible enough to handle new opportunities and new people should they come along.

JILL, 24

❝ I spent the fourth of July weekend in a tiny town in Ohio, escaping from the rat race that is Manhattan with a few friends I'd met the year before on a Caribbean cruise. After the fireworks, everyone was getting sloshed and silly, but before I joined them I got talking to a bunch of fellow New Yorkers who had randomly ended up in the same backwater. One of them had just opened an exclusive Soho boutique, frequented by celebrities. As a magazine writer, this wasn't just great for my fashion pages but for the gossip pages, too. Luckily, we both had our BlackBerries and business cards, and we pencilled in a lunch back in the city for the following week. It just shows that you never know who you're going to find where. I still use the discount card she gave me on that night out in Ohio! **9**

4 Follow the leader

Once you've made good contacts, nurture them. I had a fabulous lunch with a photographer recently. I commented on how long and luscious her lashes were. The next day, she biked round to me some Maybelline mascara with a note: 'Share my secret, next time I see you we'll both have amazing lashes.' How thoughtful, and funny. I'll always go an extra mile and reply to her emails quickly from now on. Thoughtful, polite and individual gestures really help you to stand out from other people. Even if sending make-up seems a bit over the top, a 'nice to meet you' email, note or phone call is always appreciated and sets you apart from the rest. At the very least, it means that your new contact has all your details, should they ever want to get hold of you (and you had forgotten to hand them your business card when you met, tut tut).

Everyone likes to feel important and appreciated – even the most high-and-mighty people in the world! As well as that initial contact, keep in touch and keep people updated. You'll be on their radar should any opportunity come up, rather than the contact who was out of sight, and out of mind. And remember: if you do hear on the grapevine that they have put in a good word for you, send another brief thank-you note – or even a gift if their tip came off!

5 Patience is a virtue

Yes, you are the greatest thing since David Beckham's legs but you need to give the world a chance to realise that. Don't feel disheartened or discouraged if you don't see immediate results from your increased social activity. Just stay polite and persistent. Don't sulk, and certainly don't stalk. The fruits of your labour will flourish, but not immediately and not instantly (unless you really are lucky and in the right place at the right time). Just stay organised and interested and you will see the fruits of success. Keep a record of where you've been and an address file of who you've met. Make a file on your computer to update contacts and points you need to remember about them, so that when they do call you'll be on the ball. Networking is not a short-term fix to a bad week at work; it's a long-term career plan.

6 Quality not quantity

As with all the good things in life – friends, lovers, chocolate, members of Take That – it's quality not quantity that counts. You can't be loved by all the people, all the time. And you can't possibly maintain a high standard of contact with thousands of acquaintances – it's better to maintain an amazing level with ten or 20. This is also true when you first meet new people at an event: aim for five deep-and-meaningfuls, not 50 hasty introductions and chats about the weather. Save time by wearing a name tag (if they're offered) and swapping business cards with people you wish you'd had more time to talk to – as well as those you met and found interesting.

7 Lights, camera, action!

You're in a room, you're working it, and you're fabulous. Keep the pace up, stay pro-active, and make time to do it all. Good networking takes a lot of energy and effort. You need to stay organised, groomed, updated, and of course you need to be out there. Networking needs to be ongoing – like going to the gym or getting your nails done. Don't give up after a nasty comment or an awful interview. Keep your energy up.

8 On target

Keep your eye on the ball and don't stray from your mission. If you're confused by where to start, actually make a list, or draw a diagram of your contacts and what area of your life they fit into, as well as how each area could work with another area to everyone's benefit. You may be thinking at this point, 'I don't have a network', so putting all your friends and acquaintances down on paper will really help. As I've said, you never know where your next job is going to come from, or from whom. So make your list of current 'networking people', then make a targeted list of what and who are missing from the list – and go about changing it. If it means joining committees, taking extra qualifications or throwing a party, do it. Address the places where you have gaps and fill them. If this means fewer nights at the pub, and more nights attending the staff council, do it – even if it's just for six months to get to know everyone and what their missions are.

9 Be professional, not confessional

You'll be meeting impressive people, and people who will make your life a lot easier in the future – so treat them with the respect they deserve. Ask for advice; don't beg for a job. Offer your contacts a smile, eye contact and a firm handshake. Ask your contacts for only one thing at a time – it's not their responsibility to sort out your life for you. Attend meetings on time (other people's minutes are as valuable as your own). Always thank someone for help and give credit where credit is due. Don't lie or compromise other people if they've recommended you to a friend. Don't rest on your laurels and expect your contacts to do all your work for you. If someone gets you a job – or even an interview – you owe it to him or her to prove yourself ten times over. The basic rule is being professional, not pathetic. Prove that you're worth your solid reputation.

10 Instant karma

What goes around comes around … which is a saying I take more and more comfort from as I climb the corporate ladder and have to deal with more bad will and nasty competition. There will always be some people battling their own demons and willing you to fail but as long as you handle yourself and your good friends and colleagues with respect and understanding you will reap the rewards.

So if you want to have your emails replied to, reply to other people's. If you need someone to answer your call, leave a polite and clear message. If you want nurturing and encouragement from your seniors, think about guiding and listening to people further down the ladder than you. You never know – one day, they could be the CEO of your company. The higher up the career ladder you go, the more you'll realise that everyone knows everybody else. Your reputation does precede you – so make sure it's a good one. If you are rude, condescending, bigheaded, or, let's say, fictitious with your accomplishments, people will know about it. Industry insiders love to gossip – and gossip is seldom pleasant or full of praise. Spend less time worrying what others around you are doing and more time on being the best you can.

Things to avoid

Networking is the number-one way to find a job – and not just any job, but your dream job. However, it shouldn't feel like hard work, even if you're shy or tired, or feel like you should be rewarded with a job purely on your merits and that everyone should know what those merits are by now!

People aren't psychic so you have to sell yourself – but think about these things first:

◆ **Don't cold-call people** – a good networker calls on people she knows, and asks them for the right kind of introductions. Cold-calling leaves you open to gossip, news of your enquiries will get back to your boss and, of course, without a friend's recommendation you're probably wasting your time anyway.

◆ **Don't be too formal** – networking should be fun. When you call someone for contacts or advice it should be on an informal level; you shouldn't behave as if you're at a business meeting.

◆ **Emails are fabulous,** quick, easy and convenient – but for a personal touch, picking up the phone or writing a letter are normally more effective, and they show you've gone that extra mile.

- ◆ **You've forgotten your business cards** – what a waste of a great and unexpected meeting on the train, in a club, in the queue at Starbucks. Don't forget to chuck a few in your purse at all times. Or at the very least, memorise your email address.

- ◆ **Never come straight out and beg for a job** – unless your boss really is a tyrant and you have to escape before you try to end your life with the office stapler! Just ask for suggestions, contacts and advice in the right places – and if you are qualified and hard-working, the people you're asking for advice will soon mention your name in the right circles.

- ◆ **People aren't stupid.** If you suddenly start calling an old friend from college who you've just read about in the local paper (after his huge promotion) he'll know you're not ringing to give him your congratulations, but to try and jump on his bandwagon! Make friends and contacts before you need then, and maintain them for when you do need help – either in the workplace or socially.

- ◆ **Don't be shy or afraid to ask for help** – you can't network on your own, just do so politely.

- ◆ **Don't bore people with irrelevant facts.** Take the opportunity to meet new people and find out where the right places to be are, but don't bore them with your life story. Yawn.

- ◆ **Forgot to say thank you?** More fool you! Your contacts won't be so keen to help in the future if they feel you've taken advantage of their goodwill and generosity. Don't forget to buy them a drink next time you're out, or send over a bouquet of flowers. If you don't contact them again until next time you need something, hackles will rise!

◆ **Don't pass up on opportunities to network.** Even if it's raining, snowing or the event is miles away and the venue will be full to the brim with strangers, push yourself! You can't network in front of the television with a tub of Häagen-Dazs in your hand.

RUTH, 29

❝ There's a guy in my friendship circle who thinks the world owes him a living. He's fun and a good bloke to have at the pub, but I can't shake off the feeling that he's taking us all for a ride. Not only is he lazy (we always have to work around him) and mean (I don't think he has ever bought me a drink or a birthday card) but also he resents our success. A mutual friend got a well-deserved, fabulous promotion a few months back, and all he could say was 'Gimme an interview, I want some of that cash!' He was pestering a lovely guy who now feels under pressure to sort this fool out – rather than recommending efficient, worthy people to work for his expanding company. ❞

How aggressive is too aggressive?

When people think about networking they conjure up images of inviting ex-colleagues who've landed on their feet out to dinner, or grabbing a ten-minute coffee with the new girl in accounts.

I took this a step further – and became a bit more aggressive and forthright – a few years ago, when, although I had an impressive job title and a good salary at a respected publication, I was basically miserable. All jobs have stressful periods, and there will always be personality clashes, but when you stop being able to sleep properly or you start to develop stress symptoms such as stomach aches or hives (as had happened to me) you know it's time to move on. And the quickest way to do this is to help yourself out – and put yourself out there.

The first thing you should do in a similar situation (as I did) is to make a list of all your closest allies with similar work backgrounds, and good contacts themselves. Hit the phone. Call them, and ask if you can take them out for coffee (taking all your contacts out for lunch or dinner gets pricey, and besides, most people's time out of the office is valuable – and for family and relaxation).

Pin down as many people as you can for coffee in the next seven days. Don't let things slide into next month or, even worse, 'some time soon'.

When you meet, don't be downbeat and depressed – and don't throw a bunch of CVs on the table. Simply ask about the industry, explain you are keen to move on, and ask if they've heard of anything coming up. Don't let something slide – if they mention something in passing, get the details. In fact, try to leave each meeting with at least three new contacts to chase up (always mention where you got the details from when you make contact with a friend's contact, of course).

I got about four useful contacts from these initial meetings. I sent each of them a very neat, precise CV (more of this in Chapter 8) and a polite covering letter, telling them where I had got their details from and asking for a few minutes of their time. I finished the letter by saying I would call in a few days to see if a meeting was convenient.

Normally about half the letters you send out and the follow-up calls you make will get a response. Indeed, I had two meetings on the back of these letters – and was offered two jobs. I sent my job enablers a bottle of champers each! And then carefully chose the job that was right for me – not the one with the biggest benefits' package, but the one with the best management structure and work-life balance.

This is as aggressive as you should go. You should be confident, to the point and assertive; you shouldn't be confrontational or a menace. I was unhappy so I aggressively searched for contacts and followed them up, but rather like a swan gliding across a lake, to everyone else I looked calm and was acting with dignity, they couldn't see the manoeuvres I was having to make under the water to get me heading in the right direction.

NB Often, when you are collecting more and more contacts, names will start to overlap. This could mean your friends are all attracted to the same industry people, or, more likely, that these really are the people to befriend! When you first get them on the phone, flatter them sincerely – tell them that various people have said they were the person to talk to. Everyone loves a genuine compliment.

Next level networking

Now the bad stuff is out the way, we can focus on the key resources you need in place to become the next Lynne Franks, Anita Roddick – or Paris Hilton. If you can put this advice into practice, you'll soon be running the world (if you want to, that is). Some high-level networking can help you to:

◆ Increase your visibility within your chosen field.

◆ Find you a mentor.

◆ Increase business leads that turn into profitable opportunities.

◆ Highlight you for promotion.

◆ Allow you to help out the company and improve its strategy.

◆ Make you more visible in a changing job market – and get headhunted.

A networker's guide to bonding

When you're faced with a stranger, it's easy to let the conversation turn to the simple and stress-free things in life – the weather, the lift, and the drinks …

But, if you can up the ante a little, you're likely to bond over some joint cause or pleasure, and you will then stick firmly in their mind. This will also give you a reason to contact them again when something on the subject you shared comes up: a festival, a newspaper article, a celebrity commenting on it, and so on. Start a networking file that will include not only contact details but also little facts like this that could help you out in the future.

When looking for something to start and maintain dialogue with, think:

◆ **Favourite country or type of holiday.** I'm obsessed with a cruise line called Silversea and you won't believe the

amount of contacts I've made, just by sharing my love
with fellow cruisers!

◆ **Hometown or county, or old school or university** – share
those roots and alumni information.

◆ **Favourite novelists or style of books** – you can send a
copy of a favourite with a note as a gift after meeting, or
email them about new releases.

◆ **Favourite musicians or genres of music** – again send a
CD or an iPod recommendation.

◆ **If you bond over a truly unusual hobby,** you're made! A
love of embroidery, photography, wine tasting, and so
on, is something that will make you stand out and maybe
also open up the possibility of spending more time together in the future.

DANI, 33

❝ I am now best friends with my scary ex-boss. She has a
grand reputation for being strong, ambitious, driven and for
not suffering fools gladly. And she adores me, nurtures me,
and always thinks of me if there is a project or party that
she hears about that could benefit me. Why? We bonded
through our love of New Kids on the Block. At a drunken
office party ten years ago I confessed I had been a member
of their fan club when I was a teenager. She looked suddenly
teary, and admitted the same. A few male colleagues tried to
laugh at us, but we replied with a chorus of 'Hangin' Tough'
– and that was that! ❞

On-spec networking meetings – what you need to ask

Sometimes, you meet a new contact not just to get promotion or a new job but also to find out about a new industry, club or association. When time is limited, you need to pinpoint your needs. Try asking the following:

◆ How did you get into this industry/club?

◆ How do you balance this with your personal time?

◆ Is it stressful?

◆ Is it easy to get in or join?

◆ What do you like/dislike the most about it?

◆ What does the future hold?

◆ What advice would you give to someone trying to get involved?

◆ Is there anyone you think I should speak to?

Secrets of Success

◆ The key to great networking is to be the person everyone remembers. And not for doing knickerless cartwheels after a few too many drinks, but for being brilliant.

◆ When becoming a better networker, remember the three I's: be Interesting, be Interested and be Intelligent.

◆ When you need to get the most out of an event, get there early and plan to leave late.

◆ Select a few key associations or clubs and participate in them fully and happily.

◆ Follow up on leads. You know that if you throw a dog a bone you expect him to run and catch it.

◆ Be helpful – you're not just there to take what you can. Share information and resources (with non-competitors, of course) and you'll be remembered for your openness and generosity.

◆ Stay in touch – sounds simple, and it's something we say almost as a throwaway at the end of a meeting, but do it. It works. You should be there for the good, the bad and the ugly, not just when you need something. If you have 50 good contacts, but don't contact them for a year, lots of them will be out of date and useless within that time. Send an email to check in, even if it's just on a tri-monthly basis.

◆ Never give up. Even if no one can help you immediately, every friend made is a friend for the future. Even if they just help you out with a good yoga instructor at the moment, in the future they may be able to recommend your boyfriend for a career change, and so on.

◆ If you're prone to procrastinate, set yourself a strict target of, say, collecting 100 business cards by the end of the year, or signing up to at least one beneficial extra-curricular activity.

◆ Constantly update and maintain your contacts info – keep an eye on industry movements and send good luck cards to friends in the business, or websites that could prove helpful to other people.

◆ Plan to allocate a few hours a week to networking. Whether this is by attending an office meeting, going to a cocktail party, or reading a business magazine.

◆ Always show appreciation for any help given – the more unusual the gift or funny the letter, the better.

Chapter Five

The charm offensive

THE CHALLENGE OF NETWORKING extends well beyond the office walls. As discussed, if you're good at it, you will be networking with friends, ex-colleagues, on the bus, in the spa – in your sleep, almost. This chapter is all about perfecting your behaviour outside the conference room and in society as a whole. You will be a social butterfly!

How to be the perfect guest

The key thing is to treat other people, their events and their homes with respect. Make yourself at home for sure but don't treat their homes or events like a hotel. The best guests are those who understand that welcoming anyone into their event is time-consuming and expensive. Be pleasant, easy-going and offer to help out. If you want to have a great time as a guest – and be invited back on other occasions – do the following:

◆ Don't make surprise visits to people's homes, or show up to events without RSVPing. When replying to an invitation, state a clear yes or no. No maybes! If you can't make it at the last minute, inform your host immediately.

◆ Don't arrive at an event over an hour early or an hour late without calling with a warning. If early, your hosts could be naked. If late, dinner could be burned. Neither option is appealing.

◆ Do bring an appropriate 'plus one' if invited to – don't show up with a friend if not.

◆ Do take a gift. A bottle of wine, a box of chocolates or flowers are lovely. Something thoughtful and personal, like photos or a CD or book, is even better.

◆ If invited on a tour of the property, accept it – even if you're comfortably nestled in your chair by the fire next to the tub of Quality Street. It's an honour and should be treated as such. But don't pass rude comments on your host's decor or cleanliness. And certainly don't take yourself off on a tour when not invited to do so. I was caught drunkenly snooping in someone's bedroom once – it was embarrassing all round. My story that I was looking for the bathroom wasn't believed.

◆ Don't help yourself to food or drink without being offered, unless the host has said to do so.

◆ Never show up to an event drunk.

It'll be all right on the night

If you observe these top ten tips for being the perfect invitee, you'll soon be getting invited to all the hottest tickets in town. All of the below take little effort, just some thought and care:

1. Be punctual, helpful and generous – bring a gift.

2. Be sociable – introduce yourself to other guests if the host is busy.

3. Don't be a madam. It's rude to try to upstage the host. This is their evening.

4. Be genuinely complimentary: flatter anything you love, be it the decor, cocktails, and so on.

5. Be socially acceptable. Do not tell racist, sexist or homophobic jokes. Ever.

6. Get merry and bubbly. Not pissed.

7. Be aware of people's needs. If the host needs help clearing the table, volunteer. If it's past midnight and the host has looked at the clock twice and yawned, leave.

8. Shut your mouth and let others get a word in – the universe does not revolve around your thoughts, opinions and holiday plans.

9. If it's supposed to be a fun, social evening, don't discuss the office or aggressively network all night. Having a laugh is a different kind of networking.

10. Befriend the fellow guest who looks a bit lonesome. You know how scary going out alone can be sometimes, take them under your wing to give the host one less thing to worry about. And you never know who the shy guest knows, and what they can do for you ...

NB The morning after – or at least within a week – you should text, email or send a letter to the host and thank them for a wonderful time. It is an effort to throw a dinner or party, or to organise a grander event, and praise and thanks are gratefully received. I know how, when I've held dos in the past, I've loved battling through my hangover and the washing-up with a constant buzz of 'well done' texts coming through on my mobile.

Returning the favour

When you've received exceptional hospitality, as well as sending a note of thanks, it's nice to extend an invitation in return. If your apartment isn't large – or suitable – enough for a soirée, offer to take your host (and their partner if appropriate) out to dinner, and insist on paying the bill. This is a good way to get a regular social communication set up, without either of you feeling the pressure always to be the host.

A great friend of mine has a bar/disco room in her basement, and she is always expected to throw a party (at great expense and hassle) on any special occasion – be it her birthday, a friend's birthday, a bank holiday weekend or an important football match. She is a great host and loves the attention but has recently confessed she wished someone else would occasionally take the brunt of everyone's social needs.

This year, for her thirty-first birthday, the pressure was taken off – and it was a total surprise! She disappeared for a ladies' lunch, and on her return saw over the fence into her back garden a host of busy little elves setting up a BBQ and bar – and a bouncy castle. Knowing that everyone else normally relied on her for all social events, made their effort even more special.

HOW TO PERK YOURSELF UP AT A WORK EVENT

- Splash water on your face.

- Grab some fresh air outside.

- Move about a bit – even hit the dance floor.

- If someone is suggesting coffee, grab one.

- Reapply your lipstick and have a squirt of perfume.

- Allow yourself to talk to your friend from accounts for a bit (it's still work, just a bit more like a girly gossip).

- Flirt – subtly – with the sexy waiters catering the event.

- Visualise yourself old and grey and looking back to your party-fuelled youth.

- Hum the Jon Bon Jovi mantra: 'I'm gonna live while I'm alive and sleep when I'm dead', and promise yourself a guilt-free lie-in at the weekend.

How to make a run for it!

When you need a quick – and polite – escape route from a dire event, try a few white lies and a shift of blame: you've got a headache, your friend has had an emergency (don't be too specific – bad karma and all that), or blame a dictatorial boss or mean fitness instructor while eyeing your watch nervously. Before you leave, make sure you've said hello to all the important people – be they your family, friends or colleagues, or future employers, and thank the host. If your courage fails, wait for the first person to leave then swiftly follow in their tracks.

Sadly, when you are out on the town being sociable for a work event, you may have to grin and bear it. I was at a party my magazine was throwing in Los Angeles once. I was jet-lagged, had flu and had to get up for a 5.00 a.m. flight back to New York the next day. My bed was calling me ... I could hear the crisp cotton hotel sheets calling my name. But could

I make a run for it? No! Because my boss was there, and the general rule is that unless your boss says otherwise, you have to stay until after he or she leaves. Grrrr ...

SARAH, 38

❝ I have a foolproof (if a little naughty) trick for getting out of events early when I'm tired and want an early night. I search about for the yawner, or the person who has kept their coat on, get chatting, then volunteer to share a taxi or walk with them to the bus stop. When the cab pulls up, I'll tell my host regretfully I have to leave, and that I'm looking after sleepy-pants in the corner. The host normally feels sorry that I have to leave so soon but thinks what a decent girl I am. ❞

One more night ...

Keeping sane and sober for one dinner party at someone's house should be easy, but when you're staying a few nights it's harder to conceal your real self. The answer? Learn to behave. And learn to accept house rules. As a guest, you have no right to join in family arguments, opine on the decor of the kitchen or moan about the puppy affecting your allergies. Sorry! And more than that, you need to:

◆ Show total gratitude and respect for their home and belongings.

◆ Take a gift, however small (a tin of cookies, a candle, and so on).

◆ Keep tidy. Take your things to your designated room and don't leave umbrellas, coats and bags hanging around the hallway.

◆ Be sensitive to your hosts' needs. Make yourself scarce if you sense tension or that they need an early night. Be sociable if they ask you to join them in a bottle of wine. And don't invite others back to stay the night without checking first, or expect your host – as well as playing innkeeper – to be a taxi driver.

◆ Fit in with the routine of the home. After official bed-time, don't play loud music or stay up watching television for hours, and don't surface in the afternoon and lounge around in your pyjamas expecting to get a full English breakfast. Don't spend too long in the bathroom, and if you use up all the hot water, tell someone!

◆ Be thoughtful. When you leave for the day, ask if they would like anything to be picked up on your return. Volunteer to go to the supermarket. Offer to make dinner one night. Treat your host to a takeaway. Change the bed sheets when you leave.

Accidents might happen

It's hard to maintain a sophisticated, pleasant air when you're living in close proximity to people – especially when they're not your family, who have normally seen you at your worst already. But if you want to be invited back, you have to play by the rules. You shape up, or you ship out. Natural disasters can hit you when you're staying with someone for an extended amount of time. Just a few of the mortifying things that have happened to me include spilling red wine on a cream carpet, a flush breaking on the toilet leaving me unable to clean the toilet, bumping into a friend's husband naked on the stairs at 4.00 a.m. and hearing some friends having very loud sex. Cringe.

The thing to remember is that we all make mistakes, and not to get too stressed about them – you'll all laugh about it someday. It could be worse.

The perfect guest for all occasions

Keep to a few basic rules and you will be the perfect guest par excellence, no matter what the occasion.

Being the perfect wedding guest

Arrive on time, and quietly. No one wants you causing a scene – even if you are the usual centre-of-attention, drama queen of the group! Only bring a 'plus one' if you have replied and your request has been accepted. Don't complain about the table you're on and try to swap with someone. Never mention that the food was cold/disgusting/late, and so on – the couple will be stressed as it is, complaints about the food could send them over the edge. Don't moan about being tired and leave before the speeches. Everyone should stay for the first dance, and then slip away elegantly rather than making a scene. And smile. This is the biggest day of the bride and groom's life and it has cost them a lot of money!

BELINDA, 32

❝ I returned from a trip to India and went straight from the airport to a wedding at a family home. Flying and foreign food had left me a little ill and I rushed straight to the toilet. After unloading quite a lot I was devastated to find the flush didn't work – and there was someone knocking on the door to come in. I had to think quickly. Don't hate me, but I fished out my number two with a hand towel and hid it in a cupboard. Sheer panic drove me to it, and it seemed a good idea at the time – until I heard the bride's mother had been devastated when the family dog unleashed it the day after the wedding ... when the in-laws were bonding over a day-after brunch. I've never owned up, of course. It's a Miller–Heller family mystery. ❞

Being the perfect holiday guest

When you're going on holiday with a group, or even another couple, tempers can easily flare – it must have something to do with the extreme temperatures. Also, people look forward to a break from work for so long, so if their expectations aren't met they are left feeling disappointed and this can lead to bad moods and arguments. When you're on holiday with others, take it as a chance to lean back, relax and not have to make decisions. Remove yourself from the fraught planning and worrying, and go with the flow – it you don't fancy something, simply say thanks but no thanks or take a risk and go with it. Holidays are the perfect opportunity to try something new that at first you think sounds awful. I'd never have started skiing if I hadn't been pushed and persuaded into it by a friend … and now it's my favourite thing (well, the après-ski is if I'm totally honest, but you get my (snow) drift!).

Being the perfect 'plus one' guest

We've all been invited to things as someone's 'plus one' – be it a boyfriend, platonic male friend or a girlfriend who can't be arsed to beg a man to attend her office party with her when she'd have more fun with a girlfriend. When you're a 'plus one' you should be careful not to do anything your friend would find embarrassing, this includes telling funny stories about her to her boss, her in-laws-to-be or her new spinning class. Only talk about how wonderful your social partner is and watch what you say in general – you won't know who everyone is! Don't outstay your welcome (leave when she or he does) and thank the host for your plus-one evening.

Being the perfect 'new girlfriend' guest

Meeting your beloved's parents for the first time is very, very scary. Hopefully they'll make it easy for you by being kind and welcoming. They must be wonderful, as they raised the wonderful man you're dating, right? Wrong! Boyfriends' parents can be a nightmare, but play safe by taking a nice gift, complimenting their home, listening to all their tales of Little Boy's childhood … and never mentioning sex, nudity, marriage and baby plans/fears or your past lovers.

Make it official ... being sociable on behalf of your company

Let's face it, however groomed and worthy you are normally, you can let your hair down when it's a friend's bash. However, if it's an official function related to your company, your clients, or a committee you represent, you need to pay extra attention and truly be the most stellar of guests:

1. Before you go, find out what the dress code is and stick to it.

2. Ask your boss or colleague how long you need to stay for.

3. Find out if your help is needed to set up before the official start, and whether there is anyone attending who needs to be befriended.

4. Find out if there are topics or people to be avoided.

5. Don't gatecrash an official function. This will make you look needy and desperate – and ultimately unwanted if they don't let you in. I've seen A-list stars being turned away from events they weren't included in, and, seriously, their star seems to lose a bit of its shine. If your name's not down, you're not going in. Don't push it.

Secrets of Success

◆ When at a social event where food is served, hold food in your left hand and your drink in your right. This leaves your right hand clean and greasefree for hand shaking.

◆ If you get to an event and name tags are offered, take a deep breath and wear one even if you're not keen. It's naff and a bit

1980s but you're a guest and thems the rules. It also makes for easier networking.

◆ If you've been invited to someone's house for dinner, give them plenty of notice about allergies and requirements. Serious ones. Don't expect your host to change a whole menu because you fancy going wheat-free for a week. As the good guest, you need to adapt.

◆ Don't complain about your hosts' noisy children or over-friendly pets – sadly, they're part of the package.

◆ Borrow some wellies in a sudden downpour; pinch a jumper if it gets cold, but do not expect to raid your hosts' wardrobe with total disregard. For that matter, don't raid the fridge or the drinks cabinet without permission either. It's rude.

◆ Whatever you are invited to attend, remember there really is no such thing as 'fashionably late', it's just 'I'm-an-inconsiderate-bad-guest late.'

◆ If you need more information on how to behave as a guest, think back on the things that irritated you when you were hosting a soirée and take note.

◆ Enjoy being looked after and entertained. The perfect guest is a grateful, happy guest.

Chapter Six

The hottest hostess

THE QUICKEST — AND BIGGEST — way to make an impression of the fabulous kind is to throw, host or sponsor a marvellous soirée, where the people who matter to you can relax, drink, eat and mingle in fabulous or unusual surroundings. Another way of showing your organised and kind side is to give a fabulous dinner party. Whatever the event, here's how to make it wonderful ... and here's how to cope!

Sing for your supper

Dinner parties are the greatest way to show your new boss or client that you are a multitasker, socially savvy and a great cook to boot. And it's always lovely to be invited to someone's home – it shows fondness, caring and trust. Here in Manhattan, where I live, anyone can meet up at a bar or hire a section of a nightclub, but that's dull. Staying in is the new going out in NYC, and an invite into someone's home for an intimate soirée is the hottest thing.

Yes, it can be stressful, but remember the following:

◆ You can look sweaty, tired and awful but no one will care as you've been slaving over a hot stove. And if you actually manage to look decent, people will think you're Kate Moss.

◆ Eating in means avoiding rude waiters, huge bills and taxi queues.

◆ You can choose the menu and music.

◆ You can practise your cooking and cocktail-mixing skills.

◆ Your bed is only a matter of yards away at any point!

Who to invite – and how

When sending out your invitations (a phone call or an email invite will do for a dinner party) make sure you leave enough time. If you invite people to a formal dinner a few days beforehand, they'll assume they were thought of at the last minute to fill a gap. For an informal supper party, however, any time is fine – the invitation is more like a 'Hey, come if you can' situation. When extending an invitation, ask for an RSVP by a certain date, stating their food no-nos. If you said they could bring a 'plus one', ask if they're taking you up on your kind offer and the name of their guest – especially if they're bringing someone who is extra-fabulous that you need to prepare for, or show off about!

When it comes to the guest list, getting the right mix for a dinner party is crucial. They are intimate evenings, where conversation and histories will be shared, so think carefully about who would get on with whom and amuse each other. Don't play peacemaker and invite a freshly separated couple or warring colleagues. These make-ups should be done in private and not over a bottle of Pinot Grigio with eight other people willing them on.

If the main reason for your dinner party is to impress someone you wish to network with, think even more carefully. Advise other guests about who the honoured guest is before the big night, and let them know if there are any subjects to be avoided. Tell them if your networking new friend has been recently divorced, or widowed or fired, to avoid those nasty silences. Emphasise how important it is to you that the night goes well. Avoid inviting your networking friend/couple to an evening where all the other guests are old, old friends and won't socialise particularly well. It's horrid being the only person out of the loop when the conversation rarely diversifies from 'drunken nights at uni – do you remember when …' This is funny for five minutes, then dull. It's also rude if the other guests don't open up the dining room table to more general topics of conversation.

JILL, 30

❛ When I first got together with my now ex-husband, I had to attend a variety of dinner parties with his friends from school. They were ghastly. I'd try to befriend the girls with talk of celebrities, new novels and their holidays, and they'd ignore me to tell yet another hysterical (!?) tale about them all 15 years ago. Before I knew them. And I'd never known him the way they knew him. In fact, I'd really rather rocked the boat by coming on the scene. I'd get slowly drunk while my ex pandered to them, and then defended them in the car on the way home. They – or he – never let me into the circle. And he wondered why I started to refuse to go with him, and then eventually asked for a divorce! ❜

Making dinner dynamite

Sadly, hosting a fabulous dinner party isn't all about the food. Here is a foolproof checklist of other things to prepare to make it a truly rockin' meal:

◆ Check that the table and chairs don't wobble and that your napkins and cutlery are clean and sparkling. You want your new CEO to be able to see his reflection in his spoon.

◆ Generally tidy your home, focusing on the room where you'll be eating, the kitchen and the bathroom. Spray some gorgeous fragrances and think about having some fresh flowers.

◆ Plan an area for visitors' coats, umbrellas, bags and boots, and so on. If you don't have a hall cupboard, laying things in your bedroom is fine – just check you've put away all personal items.

◆ Draw up a seating plan, if you're determined to keep your future investor away from your sister's rather creepy husband. Put out names on the table, perhaps with an added touch like a little gift, or a name painted on a candle, flower or shell.

◆ Don't rely on your guests to bring enough booze to see you through the evening. Stock up on water, soft drinks, red and white wine, and perhaps a bottle or two of champers to start the night off with – this will make everyone feel special and glamorous.

◆ If you're going to allow smoking, provide ashtrays and candles. If you want people to venture outside, make it appealing with chairs and cushions.

◆ Music should be thought out carefully. No 'Smack My Bitch Up' by the Prodigy please! Think more along the lines of Jamie Cullum and Katie Melua, early Beatles, crooning Frank Sinatra and Dean Martin, or soft and lovely classical. Once you've made your selection, set up the CDs near the stereo or programme the playlist into your iPod, and think about the right volume – it needs to be enough to fill those early awkward silences but not overbearing when the conversation starts flowing.

◆ Looking glam and cooking are not mutually exclusive, just tricky. Plan your outfit before you start in the kitchen. One hour before guests arrive, stop for half an hour to wash, dress and do your hair and make-up. Then return to the culinary finishing touches with half an hour to spare.

SUSANNAH, 32

❝ I could have killed my partner the other day. He had just moved jobs and wanted us to throw a dinner for his new team and boss. I was having a hellish time at work and wasn't too into the idea – a weekend of comfort food and television would have been better – but it was important for him to make a good impression so we went ahead. We agreed to be at home at 6.30 p.m. to start tidying and cooking. He got caught at work until 7.30 p.m., when he returned sweaty and leapt into the bathroom. I had to shop, clean and prepare, and didn't have time to change or shower. When HIS guests arrived at 8.00 p.m., he was upstairs dressing and I had to meet and greet and pour the drinks and sort the music on my own. We should have prepared more the night before, and he should have been more organised. ❞

Hosting horrors

Tut, tut – don't make silly mistakes. A modern hostess with the mostest should always:

◆ Introduce her guests, even if she thinks they have met before.

◆ Accept the offer of help if she genuinely needs it, or feels someone is offering a helping hand to have a good chat or avoid another guest.

- Keep drinks replenished, and nibbles if the dinner is delayed.

- See Susannah's story of resentment above. Give the co-host (if there is one) a suitable list of concerns.

- Keep your make-up bag in the downstairs loo for a quick freshen up.

- Don't feel you have to offer the chocolates or wine a guest has brought, unless they specifically ask you to try them or you don't have an alternative to offer.

- Don't make a big deal about clearing up. Tell guests not to worry, even if they offer. Unless they chase you down with a tea towel, they don't mean it. Leave them to relax, and you can do it in the morning while listening to the radio. If you are laid-back about the evening then your guests will be, too.

Your treasures, others' trash

You adore your children – they are mini versions of you with cute faces and endearing characteristics. But children are never that appealing when they are not your own. Remember this. If you're having people over, bribe your offspring to stay upstairs with a DVD and a takeaway. Even send them away to Grandma's for the night!

Pets are also less adorable to your visitors than to you. You may think it's sweet that your dog humps your leg or that your cat leaps onto the kitchen worktops. But others won't. Especially if they're allergic to them. Only unleash your pets if everyone – and I mean everyone – is begging to meet them. Not everyone thinks animals are magic. Also, it's not enough just to remove the cat or dog – remove their hair and their litter tray, too. And ask someone before the event if your home smells. If so, get that incense out, animal-lover!

Wok 'n' roll!

With the other matters under control, we now have to get you going with your cooking.

There are ten golden rules when embarking on a menu to impress and satisfy:

1. **Don't go mad.** In the kitchen, being over-ambitious rarely pays. Keep your big ideas for the conversation – when talking about the great ideas you have to take the company forward, for example. A simple chicken casserole done well is better than sweet-and-sour dumplings done badly.

2. **Practise making the meal before the big occasion** – preferably on someone who will be honest but encouraging.

3. **Make sure one course is very easy.** Choose something that can be prepared the night before, like a delicious soup or Key lime pie, for example. Freeze it, if necessary.

4. **Cheatin' eatin'.** If the idea of doing a three-course dinner really terrifies you, visit your local supermarket and spend, spend, spend on the ready-made dinner party specials. Some are so fabulous they taste like restaurant food, and it's easier and not much more expensive than making things from scratch. Glam up with fresh herbs, fruits and cheeses. And don't feel you have to admit your sin. Just hide the packaging carefully. If someone pesters you for the recipe though, 'fess up! Your guests will admire your supermarket savvy!

5. **Make one course non-cook friendly:** cheese and biscuits, fresh fruit salad, Caesar salad, antipasto, and so on.

6. **Don't take any chances.** Keep some takeaway numbers on hand in case of an emergency.

7. **Don't shop in a panic.** Sit down with a cup of tea and list everything you will need (remembering ice and lemon for drinks, nibbles, after-dinner chocolates, and so on).

8. **If you're not used to hosting huge happy soirées,** stick to a guest list of six on the first few occasions.

9. **Timing is everything.** Have interesting bite-size treats ready when guests arrive, then allow 30 minutes for them to eat the first course. Time the main course to be on the table an hour from when you put the starter down. When it comes to dessert, ask guests when they fancy eating. If it's cold, like cheese and fruit, it can be simply left for people to pick at when and if they fancy. When there's a lull in the conversation and you want to get people moving, offer coffee.

10. **Don't get tipsy until the main course has safely arrived in front of your guests.** As soon as they've tucked in, kick back and enjoy yourself a little. You deserve to! Bon appétit.

NB Sometimes – no matter how great the food is – a dinner party just doesn't get going. If you're worried your party is turning into a social Siberia, keep the booze flowing and turn the music up. Tell some jokes, flatter everyone, get your camera out and get people posing, open some windows to get the air circulating, pull out a popular board game ... or admit defeat and offer to get people's coats.

Guests that make you go 'Grrrrrr ...'

Not everyone you invite to your home will be pleasant, sociable and exciting. How do you handle the troublemakers? Well, you can't be rude; remember that things may seem exaggerated to you because you're so stressed.

Smile at guests who show up empty-handed, and thank the Lord you're not so mean. If people are late for dinner, don't let it eat you up. Delay your plans for the expected half an hour then go ahead and serve without them. They may have lost their manners but you haven't lost your meal to the bin. Guests that arrive too early are just as bad if you're not ready for them. Plonk them in the lounge with a drink and a bowl of treats and act like they're not there.

If guests start to argue, diffuse the situation by offering another round of drinks or suggesting a move into another room. If a guest gets too drunk, try coffee and five minutes of fresh air outside. If that fails, order a taxi. If they can't even get into a taxi, shove them in the guest room with a pint of water.

Cocktail queen

If you can't cope with the idea of a full-on, sit-down dinner, go for throwing a drinks party instead. Gathering networking pals together for a few bevvies is much cheaper and easier, and it's less stressful. You can spend less time with your head in the fridge and more time being a truly fabulous cocktail (mover and ...) shaker! Just avoid the cheese straws, snowballs and slow dances with your colleague's husband.

THE PERFECT COCKTAIL PARTY

- By tradition, cocktail parties are short and sweet. How marvellous. Throw yours between 7.30 and 9.30 p.m. Don't drag it out or people will get hungry and drunk. Cocktails can be lethal.

- Don't go mad with the drinks cabinet. The key word is elegant. You want to impress people so choose a theme or colour scheme. Buy enough ingredients to provide four cocktails each.

- Make life interesting for the teetotal guests and designated drivers. Stock up on water and interesting fizzy drinks and research a non-alcoholic cocktail. Make some flavoured ice, or ice frozen with berries and edible flowers.

- Some strange dudes (mostly men, the same men who don't understand *Sex and the City*) don't like cocktails. Supply beer for such philistines.

- Theme cocktails to special occasions and seasons. Eggnog and mulled wine at Christmas, chocolate Martinis at Easter ...

- Remember: long cocktails last longer – and get people less drunk. Don't offer too many shots. Avoid things that need more than four ingredients – they'll get more and more complicated as people get more and more tipsy!

- Make the bash invitation and RSVP specific if you don't want waifs and strays. Have a strict 'plus one', not 'plus posse' policy.

- Ban invitees from bringing their children and dogs – they take up valuable space and can prove to be a menace.

- Music should be low key and interesting – retro, samba, salsa, hotel mixes, cover versions, and so on.

- Although the focus is on the drinks, if you're hosting an event on a week night people will be coming famished straight from work. Serve something simple. Nothing that requires a great deal of time, money or staff. Delicious breads, cheeses, olives, tomatoes, dried meats and fruits always go down well. Chocolate-dipped strawberries and fortune cookies are fun – serve them on interesting trays. I love to serve canapés on mirrors, strewn around the edges with glitter.

- Pick the venue carefully. If your home is too small to swing a cat in, let alone a dancing partner, move the soirée on to somewhere more suitable: the upstairs of your favourite restaurant, a room in a local nightclub, your parents' garden, for example.

- With a drinks party, you're saving cash on food but normally inviting more guests, so the bill can still add up. You have to be prepared to spend money. Rather than cutting corners, I suggest inviting fewer people.

Dare to be different

By now, you will have been to thousands of soirées, discos, weddings, office parties, and so on. They can all start to blend into one. However fun these events are supposed to be, they can be as dull as watching paint dry if the right elements (people, food, drinks, music, decor and buzz) don't fall into place.

Never be scared to be exciting and different. As long as the basic elements listed above are in place, have fun. Experiment with mad decorations, games, lighting, gift bags, table decorations, canapés, entertainment, and so on. Think about serving breakfast bacon rolls at midnight to send everyone on their way, have a mini firework display, give out party bags with balloons and streamers, cover the ceiling in fairy lights and cover surfaces in sparkly confetti, hire a karaoke machine, or, if the budget allows, a special performer. Hire coloured glasses and have fun things for the drinks, such as umbrellas, flowers, straws and frozen cooling cubes that light up.

A night to remember

No two nights out are the same, so you must adapt your hostess-with-the-mostest formula for each and every event. Sometimes things will be low key and relaxed, other times you'll be looking to impress your guests and you'll need to shell out extra money and time.

VIP guests

If the main purpose of your event is to woo and impress someone special, you have to give them a large portion of your time. And advise your partner – if you have one – to do the same and make an effort. Always make sure your VIP guests have a drink, and offer them the food first (before it gets cold if it should be served warm). Don't stick to their side like a stalker but make introductions to interesting, like-minded people (especially if they're likely to sing your praises), and thank them for coming when they leave.

Company cool

If you're hosting an event on your company's behalf, you need to observe the following rules very closely:

1. Arrive before everyone else to make sure the venue looks perfect.

2. Be accessible and greet all the guests as they enter.

3. Make a point of introducing key people to your boss or partner.

4. Stand back for a few seconds once an hour to observe the scene. See who looks lonely, thirsty or fed up, and sort it out.

5. This isn't primarily about you having fun, finding a date or getting drunk. Treat the night like an extension of the office – you're representing yourself and the company.

Networking nights

Nothing shows more generosity and sense of fun than throwing a dinner or drinks party. Make the most of the effort you are already putting in to invite those who you've met and bonded with: ex-colleagues you used to get on with, your new team at work, your neighbours. Don't be rude or obnoxious, however stressed, tired or drunk you get. Greet everyone warmly and really only relax yourself when you can see the mood is set and your good work has paid off. Hide a bottle of champagne to open for yourself when you finally feel like, 'Hooray! I've thrown a damn good night out for everyone!'

NB However important he or she may be at work or within the committee you are trying to climb, don't include the rude, racist or rowdy on your elegant, intelligent guest list. They'll get everyone's back up and are bound to make unnecessary, nasty comments to the wrong person (such as your mother or your new boss). And don't include your 'frenemy' – the girl who pretends to like you just to get included but will spend the evening back-stabbing you and slagging off your do.

Secrets of Success

◆ The night before your bash, think about what you want to achieve. What image do you want to portray? Who do you want to befriend, and who do you want to introduce and be introduced to? And think about how to ensure the event is smooth sailing and that everyone has the maximum amount of fun – who will get on with whom, who wouldn't, suitable ice-breakers, and so on.

◆ Remember to eat something before your drinks party starts, or you'll fall over with exhaustion once you start drinking.

◆ If you're nervous about getting the party started, call on your closest, trusted friends to arrive before kick-off to build up the atmosphere.

◆ When serving drinks, allow four per person. When serving canapés, allow 10–15 per person.

◆ Don't be a tight arse. Scrimp for the rest of the month. You can't ruin an otherwise brilliant dinner by serving a nasty, cheap frozen cheesecake for dessert because the pennies have run out. Being the hostess with the mostest is an expensive business, but will be worth it for the praise and glory that will be rained upon you.

◆ Accidents will happen in your home, but try not to go berserk. Expect it. Keep cleaning materials and stain removers to hand.

◆ As the fabulous hostess, you should expect to have fun and feel proud, but you shouldn't expect to sit down and gossip all night with your oldest friends. In fact, your true friends will probably see less of you than anyone (but they'll understand).

◆ Do make the effort to look good. Buy a new dress for the occasion. Take the apron off, throw your hair out of its practical ponytail, spritz on some perfume and smile. Wow – she can cook, clean, host, and look amazing. What a modern girl!

◆ Don't think about tidying up – or how your head is going to feel – until tomorrow. You've done enough for one night!

◆ When things have calmed down a bit, think back and make notes – what music got people smiling and reminiscing, what recipe did everyone beg you for, who was wonderfully sociable, and who didn't show up after RSVPing yes? Remember it all!

Chapter Seven

The rewards of good networking

Aᶠᵗᵉʳ ᵃˡˡ your hard work, good thinking and social engagements, you deserve to reap the pleasures of your new networking skills. Yes, of course you want the better job, and to earn the respect of your peers, but what is life without a little well-earned luxury and glamour. Grab your signature sunglasses and off we go into a fabulous world of life's little pleasures.

Flying high

For work and play, the modern girl is travelling more than ever. We're expected to go on three vacations a year, and fly at least twice. It sounds glamorous ... until you're stuck between two sweaty snorers in cattle class and the airline sends your luggage to Rio de Janiero instead of where it should be (this has happened to me twice – Rio!). But travelling around the world is essential, I believe, to having an open mind and expanded views – plus a fabulous photo album filled with memories and experiences. And the chance to be a global networking phenomenon.

To make flying more bearable so that you arrive at your destination as a fabulous modern girl, not a neurotic networker, try:

◆ **Choosing a book you won't be able to put down,** long enough to last the entire flight. Time will fly. Choose the author carefully – you need to get your mind off travelling.

◆ **Carrying a fabulous pack of in-flight essentials:** a lavender spray to mist the cheap airline pillow with; a pashmina (passé in the fashion world but forever worthy while travelling); a good lip balm and face moisturiser; and a toothbrush and make-up essentials to sparkle up with

30 minutes before landing. I swear by Clarins Beauty Flash Balm.

◆ **Packing your own food,** and ignoring the airline mush, which is filled with fat and salt – and do you really need four courses anyway? Choose kindly – no strong-smelling curries to bother your row. Drink lots of water and minimal alcohol and coffee. Unless you've just got engaged and you're on the champers, you can manage to stick to soft drinks for the sake of your dehydrated skin, can't you?

◆ **Wearing the right clothes** – loose fitting, natural fabrics are best. Put a hair band and a pair of sunglasses in your carry-on bag for when you land. Avoid stilettos.

All of these tips will not only make your journey time more pleasant but will also make you seem like a professional, fabulous traveller to all around you. You never know who you will bump into at the airport; last week I bumped into a friend from NYC in Los Angeles airport on my way to San Francisco – bizarre! Also, if you're travelling for business, others will be, too. At certain times of day, everyone on the flight will be movers and shakers making their way to an important meeting or conference. Have your business card on you, and don't be scared of chatting to the people seated next to you. If they're not nice or useful and you really want to switch off, just shut them up by politely explaining you need to read something, and/or putting in your iPod.

The upper classes

Obviously, you're going to meet the biggest movers and shakers in the world if you're flying first or business class. Sadly, not many of us can afford it – and few companies provide it as a perk, unless you're flying longer than eight hours and meeting all your targets! If you are flying frequently with the same airline, sign up to their membership scheme as soon as possible. The miles really do add up, especially if you are managing to sneak in a few business-class flights. Even without the better seat on the plane, just having enough points to gain access to the airline's lounge is fabulous, and will make your flight much more bearable. You'll board feeling well fed, hydrated and chilled (some lounges even offer massages, facials and shower rooms).

JANEY, 36

❛ I've always found being friendly and polite is an international code that gets you the best deals around the world. It helps if you learn a few words in the native tongue – it shows you're treating the country with respect, and the locals really appreciate it. Also dress appropriately, and hotel staff will appreciate it. You see women wandering around hotel lobbies in bikinis and it looks awful, or families trundling through soaking wet and leaving dangerous puddles of water behind. Those people will not be getting upgraded. ❜

How to get upgraded

Ooh, the magic when the air steward tells you to turn left, not right, as you board your plane is insurmountable! The joys of leaving cattle class over your shoulder will put a smile on your face for weeks. Here are a few tips for getting into business class:

1. **Dress well.** It's an old wives' tale that just happens to be true. Sport clean, expensive-looking clothes and you'll stand out as someone who would be acceptable for an upgrade.

2. **Be polite to the person at the check-in desk.** They hear 'can I have an upgrade?' a thousand times a day – you need to stand out as deserving one. Ask quietly, don't be pushy, but make your plea: 'I've never travelled business and I'd love to see … /I have a meeting first thing and I'm worried I won't sleep/I've had a really tough week and you'd really help me out.' Say it all with a big smile.

3. **Get a note on your booking.** Ask a friend in the industry to put a request for an upgrade on for you, or call the airline in advance and say it's a landmark birthday or honeymoon, or that you're very tall and need leg room if at all available. This has happened for me. I said I was 1.8m (6ft), they heard 1.9m (6ft 3in) – and they thought they had some kind of circus-act woman on their hands – it did get me upgraded though!

4. **Never give up.** Even as you're sitting in your cramped, tiny seat at the back, make your plea (don't be embarrassed). If you're sitting next to someone incredibly large, unhygienic or loud, pray that the steward takes pity on you.

5. **Find out for next time you fly.** Question the airline staff –
   what does it take to get upgraded?

NB You can also push for upgrades when you arrive at
your destination. If the hotel is below capacity, push for a
suite or a room with a view. Join the hotel chain clubs to col-
lect points and privileges. Ask to talk to the hotel manager –
tell him you've been recommended; that you normally stay
with the rival chain; that you have friends looking for your
feedback before they book. The manager may then be
inclined to switch your room. Fill in forms when you leave so
that if you return you'll be looked after. Offer to take part in
any promotions they have; that is, pose for photos, attend a
sales talk. If your talking isn't getting you anywhere, simply
ask if there are vacancies, and how much it would cost to get
an upgrade. You will probably get a good deal.

How to network on holiday

Some of the most useful, brilliant people I've ever met I
encountered at a swim-up bar with a pina colada in my
hand. Holidays give people the great opportunity to kick
back and relax but the (sad) truth is that many of us are so
defined by our jobs that we find it impossible not to talk
about them for a week. Don't push business chat hard on
holiday, but if you find a common link (a city, a company, a
career), do discuss it, and ask for advice and opinions.
Establish if you have any mutual contacts at the beginning
to avoid saying the wrong thing. Offer to buy him or her a

drink, and include their partner and family in conversations. Swap email addresses, but don't insist on calling them the first day back in the office. Don't stick to their side in a stalking manner. Don't follow them to the beach, or be there waiting with a towel as they step out of the pool. Play it cool.

Wining and dining

The easiest way to enhance your social and work life is to eat out at good restaurants and indulge in a fine bottle of wine. What better way of networking with new colleagues or friends than over a superb three-course meal? You can make this experience even better if you are treated well and receive fabulous service. There are key ways of making sure you are looked after as soon as you enter a bistro (your boss will be impressed), here's how:

◆ Don't feel intimidated. Often we feel too shy to book the sexiest, fanciest new restaurant – fearing they won't let us in because we're not Kate Moss & Co. Not true. Your money is as good as theirs. Book a great table with a few weeks' notice; ask for the table away from the kitchen and toilets, in the centre of the room (if you want to see and be seen) or in a quiet corner (if you want quiet and romance).

◆ If it's a special event, tell the maître d'. You should expect some chilled champagne or a dessert with some candles in it, and, at the very least, special service.

◆ If you can't get a booking for dinner at the latest must-go haunt, go 'Californian' and try it out for pre-dinner drinks to scope out the place and meet the manager (and to get the lowdown to tell your colleagues), or later in the evening for coffee and dessert.

◆ If you want to get good service, don't go at the busiest times (Friday or Saturday nights); pick a lunchtime or an evening between Monday and Thursday instead.

◆ Don't expect to ring up the night before to book a table for eight people. In fact, if you book at any time for a table for over eight people, don't expect to get the best one – large groups are known to be louder so they are put somewhere were they can't disturb the other guests. If you want a truly fine dining experience, stick to four people maximum.

Tipping

If you want to be welcomed back into the bosom of a lovely restaurant – tip. It's that simple. I live in America where not tipping is regarded as poorly as shooting someone in the foot. It's not as strict in the rest of the world yet, but is still an easy way of showing your appreciation. It's catching on more worldwide now too.

HOW MUCH SHOULD YOU TIP?

• 0 per cent is only acceptable if your food has been cold, late, and wrong, and the staff have been rude and made no attempt to remedy the aforementioned.

• 10 per cent for reasonable service.

• 15 per cent for good service.

• 20 per cent for excellent food, advice, facilities and service.

Business entertaining

In the course of your high-flying career, you will expect to wine and dine clients – alone, with colleagues, or even worse, with your boss. Cringe! Remember the basics: don't talk with your mouth full; don't spit something out or make 'ugh' sounds if you don't like something (be discreet); don't take food off other's plates; don't lick your fingers; don't play with – or brush – your hair at the table; don't text or have long phone conversations at the table. Do use the right cutlery; do sip your wine; do use your napkin; and do put your knife and fork together at 'twenty-five past five' when you've finished eating. When it comes to the bill, wait a few beats to see if the most senior/rich person at the table looks to be picking it up, if not offer. Don't grab the bill and look, simply suggest 'Shall I?' with a hand gesture – that will be someone else's key to step in if they should. The basic rule when picking up the tab is that the person who planned the meeting should pay.

NB If you need to make a good impression – and keep clean and presentable – avoid eating fondues, spaghetti and tagliatelle, crab and lobster, or too much garlic.

How to socialise and network at the same time

◆ Prepare who you want to talk to, don't prepare an attack.

◆ Take your business card, not your CV.

◆ Don't focus on yourself; sell yourself with amusing stories by normal chit-chat.

◆ If you're asked, 'What do you do for a living?', have a 20-second interesting reply planned. Remember it, and use it whenever asked.

◆ Sell yourself by telling amusing, comical stories about yourself and your work history. Don't take yourself too seriously – you'll bore everyone.

Boozing ... then losing!

In your life as a fabulous executive, business drinking will become a frequent part of your social calendar. Just be careful of drinking too much and losing your dignity, your stomach or your knickers (particularly when drinking with business acquaintances). If you have overindulged, don't be swayed into the 'hair of the dog' school by evil colleagues. If you're feeling a little green around the gills the day after the night before, hydrate yourself with water and replenish your vitamin C with freshly squeezed orange juice. Stock up on carbohydrates – pasta and sandwiches are easy to stomach – to keep your energy up. You'll make it through that important meeting ... just promise yourself a hot bath and an early night.

HOW TO STAY SANE AND SOBER UP QUICKLY

1. Don't mix spirits – in fact avoid them altogether.

2. Stop drinking at midnight.

3. If you've suddenly turned into an incoherent witch, take a breather outside or in the loos.

4. Refocus, drink water, chew mint gum, eat something.

5. Get to bed. If the world is spinning, keep one foot out of bed and on the floor – it works.

6. Remember: 'Beer on wine – feel fine. Wine on beer – feel queer!'

How to get yourself on a VIP list

Securing a place on the best guest lists is purely about networking. Life is so much more wonderful – and cheaper – when you don't have to queue up and pay for admission into your town's hottest places; you can simply slip behind a velvet rope by dropping your surname. The easiest way to get on the lists is to do your research – it's the same way as you'd network in your working life. Investigate who is the promoter of the club, get to know the doorman, chat to the DJ once you're in, and ask about membership. Call in advance and ask for a guest list – tell them your birth date so you get free entry for you and your pals on your birthday. Find out about reserving a table if you promise to spend a certain amount of cash. Tip everyone well – even the lady in the cloakroom. They'll remember you fondly.

Networking time out

The fast pace and frenzy of modern life can send modern girls into a spiral of stress and tiredness. To be the best though, we need to look after ourselves – mind, body and spirit. We are worth nothing to ourselves, our friends and family, or our company, if we run ourselves into the ground. That's why little luxurious treats are so important. Money helps but it's not the be all and end all. Here are a few rewards you can give yourself to replenish your soul when you're feeling exhausted, damaged, or that you've worked your arse off and deserve to be a little selfish. Don't feel guilty about taking time out; call it networking with the most important person you know – you!

♦ You know if you're genuinely tired or feeling lazy. If you're tired, skip the gym – your cellulite won't double in a week. Forget the treadmill and head to a coffee shop for an incredibly large, fancy piece of cake and a cappuccino.

♦ Get up on a Sunday, venture out to get the papers and some bagels in your pyjamas, then climb back into bed with it all and stay there for as long as you wish.

♦ Hire out your three favourite films and watch them back to back with your best girlfriends and a bowl of treats.

♦ If your Saturday is a busy day with chores and rushing around, schedule in an afternoon nap and make sure you have it – take a hot chocolate and a good book with you for a two-hour snuggle down.

♦ Been avoiding your boyfriend and his advances lately? Sex can feel like an effort, but set time aside to reinstate your animal side. You won't regret it.

◆ Hire a cleaner. You can't do it all. Consider paying for someone to come in and tidy for you as a necessary luxury, allowing you time to relax at the weekend.

◆ Take an aromatherapy course – not only will the lessons take your mind off work, but you'll be able to use oils on yourself and in your home wisely to encourage relaxation and well-being.

◆ If your weeks seem to build momentum as they go on, with you feeling it is acceptable to stay late in the office every night or be persuaded to go out drinking, build a 'date night' into your schedule. On your date night, you look after yourself and do what you need to. Take it seriously. Don't be persuaded to change it. You come first.

NB A great trick to keep you balanced and motivated while networking is to take on the glass half full, not the glass half empty, approach. In your career, relationships and social life look and focus on the positives and work out solutions to the problems. Remember: it takes 27 facial muscles to frown, and only 13 to smile. Your life will seem much better – regardless of the hours that you have to work, or the salary you have – if you feel happy, respected, appreciative and calm. Many people I've met in my career get ahead by putting other people down. I believe the true way to get ahead is to do the opposite. Don't pay attention to what those around you are doing, unless you can learn something positive from them. You shouldn't be climbing over other people to climb the career ladder.

Secrets of Success

◆ Has networking been taking over your life recently? Holidays are the quickest way to de-stress and forget all your troubles. Don't take your job on vacation with you. You could be staying in the finest five-star hotel in the world but if you're only looking at your BlackBerry who cares if there's an infinity pool? Do a little light networking if the opportunity bites you on the arse, but don't pursue it to the detriment of your relationship and well-being.

◆ Travel light. Packing and lugging cases around makes people tetchy and tired – and no one will want to talk to you like that.

◆ Love the differences. I'm embarrassed by fellow Brits who travel abroad and demand fish and chips, shouting in English as they do so. Respect and appreciate every country and its people. You won't be making any foreign friends if you have an attitude ... and who said the only people worth networking with are your fellow countrymen?

◆ Don't feel obliged to make small talk in your hotel or on your cruise. Politely turn down offers of a drink rather than going along and resenting it. It's not selfish to look after yourself first – especially on holiday.

◆ When eating out, don't allow members of your party to be rude to restaurant staff. It will reflect badly on you. Quietly tell them to give it a rest, or take it upon yourself to solve the problem calmly. Of course, if it's your boss or a big client doing the badmouthing, you might have to keep your opinion to yourself – just distance yourself from the mischief-makers.

◆ If the designated driver has stuck to water all night, don't expect them to cough up for your expensive taste in brandy. Be fair. Any kind of thoughtlessness or meanness goes down badly – and shows you up for someone who isn't used to dining in good restaurants or hasn't got a good grip on social etiquette.

◆ Learn some diplomatic skills. Be tactful with people.

◆ If you've got a job – or got yourself into a financial position – where luxuries are more free-flowing, treat those you love. Your entourage shouldn't expect a free ride, but surprise them occasionally with the fruits of your hard labour. Take your school friend to dinner in a fabulous restaurant; treat your mum to a manicure when you're heading for yours. This is the kind of networking everyone loves!

◆ When it comes to friends and acquaintances, it's quality not quantity that counts. Don't put up with the rude, crude or undesirable just to have another phone number in your mobile. Follow your instincts; follow your heart and your head. Your life will be better for it.

◆ Appreciate the good life, and, more than that, appreciate the good people in your life. No one's perfect – but remember a lot of us are trying really hard to be decent, kind and loyal, and we need to be rewarded for that. Make sure you're in that club. Don't spend all your time networking and forgetting who really matters and who is really there for you.

Chapter Eight

Working girl

T'S ALL VERY WELL BEING THE smoothest schmoozer in town, but if your acumen and attitude in the office lets you down, it's worth nothing. While networking, you need to sparkle and shine. While in the workplace, you need to be a perfectionist, a team player and ever so motivated. Here's how to be a perfect boss, colleague and employee while carving out the best career and future for you.

Career networking

Before you even get into the office, there are a few rules to make sure you end up in the right office. And yes, they are networking rules:

1. Keep your networking web wide: include past and present colleagues, bosses, friends with similar careers, your school and college alumni, plus people you've met at networking events.

2. Keep in touch with your network – don't forget them when you're happily settled in office life. Things can change quickly and you'll need to call on them.

3. Don't just use your networking skills to get job leads. The people you meet can help you and advise you on everything from new computing systems to office politics.

4. Escape the office every now and again and get out on your work's social scene. Often, more friends are made over a gin 'n' tonic than an office-based meeting.

5. Networking isn't a one-way street. If you have seen or heard of someone good on the market, grab them. Bring

them into your company. The more talented people you have around you, the better you'll look and the easier your job will be – you might even get out of the door at a decent time!

Get yourself a mentor

I've been blessed with a series of remarkable bosses. Not all of them have been kind, diplomatic and nurturing, but some of them have possessed amazing talent, creativity and energy – and I've learned a lot from each of them. Even if while working for them I felt they were difficult or boring, looking back they all taught me a lesson to take away from the experience.

A mentor is very important when you first start work. You need someone you can go to with your questions, your fears and your successes. Search out an office soulmate who smiles and supports you, and is a few years your senior. Break the ice by treating them to a Starbucks and a muffin, and ask for some feedback on how you're doing. Don't arse-lick, stalk or get in the way, but do show your appreciation and admiration. Stick to a mentor of the same sex – otherwise people will talk.

Don't take offence at any criticism levelled at you. I had an amazing boss in my first job at a glossy magazine. She didn't mince her words. After six months of working hard, I asked for the morning off because I was going to a party the night before and I thought I might have a hangover. She pointed out it was press week and that she'd leave the decision to me. Obviously, being enthusiastic (and a little bit scared of her) I ended up not drinking and getting into work earlier than usual. On my desk sat a box of expensive chocolates and a note: 'I knew you'd make the right decision.' And I had. At that point, my career took precedence over drinking and partying.

Follow your mentors' careers even after you leave their direction, Google their career pasts, their highs and lows ... and read articles about other people in the public eye that you admire. They don't have to work in your field, as long as they have qualities you admire that you want to bring to your office and your management style.

If you hear of someone on the grapevine that you admire, don't be shy to drop him or her a line saying you've heard great things or read a feature on them, and you'd love to meet them for a chat if they ever have the time.

GETTING A BETTER JOB

1. Review and update your CV constantly. Don't make it too long but get the key points in there. Keep details of awards and qualifications.

2. Make people interested in you. Get out and about. Volunteer for committees. Prove (without showing off) that you have skills and aspirations higher than your current status. Dress for the role you want, not the role you have. Your current job is a stepping stone to something even better – with more kudos, cash and credit.

3. Go informal. Write to people in other departments, your boss, or people you respect in rival companies and ask for off-the-record chats. Don't worry if there aren't any official vacancies – just put yourself out there.

4. Don't resign in a huff and search for a job from home. As soon as you're in your pyjamas on that couch, your

motivation – and appearance – will fade, and getting yourself back in physical and mental shape will be a battle. I love the saying 'If you want something done, ask a busy person to do it.' It's true! When you're in hyper-efficient mode in the office, adding a few extra enquiring emails to your to-do list will seem like nothing. So, search for a new job while employed, however miserably.

5. Think positive. I have been fired once and I've been made redundant once. Both times were emotionally draining and personally shaming, but I stayed motivated and have never had one single day unemployed in my whole career. Don't give in to career despair. Keep smiling, planning and visualising a better working environment – and it will happen for you as it always has for me.

How to write the perfect CV

Don't feel like you have to include everything you've ever done, plus the kitchen sink in your CV. The design and content of your CV should be clean and simple. Do not get too personal (you shouldn't list your marital status, height, weight, dependants and impending lawsuits or holidays). Don't include photographs. No matter how pretty you are. Don't go into religion, race or what you like to do in bed in this document. Shhhhh …

Basically, tailor your selling sheet to the specific job and company – add and subtract as relevant. Find out as much as you can about the position before sending off your CV.

The simplest, standard flow is this:

◆ **Contact information:** address, phone numbers and email details.

◆ **Objective statement:** you don't need one, but if you feel it is important it should go here. They are useful if you are changing career paths and need to explain why, or you're quite new and don't have much of a career path to list. Be honest, impressive and make sure it links in to what you feel the company is looking for.

◆ **Professional summary:** list your skills and extra career-related qualifications.

◆ **Employment history:** clearly list dates, positions held and main responsibilities and achievements during the time with each company.

◆ **Education:** keep it brief and to the point, just list qualifications, grades, name of schools and university, and dates attended. Don't worry about anything prior to the age of 15.

◆ **Other interesting facts** ... go here, at the bottom. Only list hobbies if they are relevant (who cares if you like cross-stitch and dirty dancing). List associations, affiliations and volunteer work that are relevant to your position, or the position you want.

> **NB The covering letter is just as important as the CV.**
> This should simply state who you are, what service you pro-
> vide and how you can be contacted. Both your CV and letter
> should have immaculate spelling and grammar, and all
> addresses and titles should be 100 per cent correct. Type
> your CV and covering letters – no shoddy handwriting is
> acceptable. Use the letter to draw attention to your positives
> and explain briefly why you would be perfect for the vacancy.
> Conclude with an impressive and memorable line. And
> proofread once, and then twice for good measure.

References

Don't put 'references on request'. You must assume the
people who you are writing to for a job are very busy and
sifting through thousands of CVs. Help them, and you will
help yourself. Provide all the info so that it is there at their
fingertips. Gather references throughout your career. College tutors who you impressed, former employers who were
sad to see you go, and so on. If they will oblige, ask them to
write and sign references in advance, and post them with
your CV or take them with you on your first interview.
Make sure your references are up to date and correctly
identified, and warn someone that you are using them as a
reference. They should be someone who is still in your life,
even if just on a casual email catch-up basis.

Web CVs

We're all so modern and technical these days – and we're
getting better and better at selling ourselves on the Internet.
If we're not trying to find love on Match.com or showing

off about our lives on Myspace.com, we're throwing our CVs on the web and waiting for the dream job to come and bite us on the arse. Some friends of mine have got back into the workplace after having babies using this easy, wide-reaching route. If you decide to do this, make sure you know how to use key words, which a prospective employer will find easy to search for. It is more acceptable to include a photo, or even a relevant video as a jpeg on a web CV. To make yours stand out, ask a technical or artistic friend to design the page for you. Once you're happy with it, you can email it to companies, or link it to an employment website. Once in an interview, you can present it on your laptop. You'll certainly stand out, and prove that you're creative and computer literate.

Interesting interviews

You're selling yourself and trying to improve your future – so what makes you think you can turn up in a dirty shirt with a hangover. You must be interesting, alert, clean, smart, entertaining, honest and humble.

In fact, let's make it simple. These are the things you must not do:

1. Do not arrive late. Look up where you've got to get to and leave with 30 minutes to spare for traffic, emergency toilet trips, and so on.

2. Don't dress like a tramp. You make the greatest impact in the first 17 seconds of the interview, and in that time all the interviewer really has time to take in is your personal hygiene, your wardrobe choices and your handshake. Keep colours subdued, patterns simple and do be conservative – gold lamé mini-dresses are never good, least of all in an interview.

3. Even if your mind has gone blank and you're feeling like an extra from *Shaun of the Dead*, remember not to zombify totally. Smile, make eye contact and sit up straight.

4. Research! Why are you better than the many other qualified, charming modern girls who have applied for this job? Read up, learn the facts and prepare a few sensible, relevant questions for the end of the interview.

5. Don't smoke, drink, chew or blow gum bubbles during an interview. 'Nuff said.

6. Yes, the interviewer wants a full answer – but not *War and Peace*. Don't go rambling on and on and on. Keep your answers clear and focused. Also, on the subject of chit-chat, do not interrupt the interviewer or talk over the top of them. Make sure you listen properly to everything they say.

7. If you can't say anything nice, don't say anything at all. Keep it quiet rather than backstabbing and bitching about your current company, colleagues or boss. Moaning and nastiness will send out the wrong vibes and you're better than that.

8. When the person asks what your weaknesses are, use only the ones that can be turned around into a lesson learned or a positive. Think carefully about your qualities, skills and accomplishments to sell them without over-selling them. No one likes a show-off.

9. Fit your interview banter to the job and the company you're applying for. Practise the interview in front of a mirror or with a friend. Explain how your career history and education would benefit the company.

10. When your time is up don't just go on about your salary expectations and what kind of package you desire; you should leave the interview with a firm goodbye speech stating why you want the job and why you'd be brilliant at it. And, again, a good, firm handshake.

HOLLY, 29

❝ In my job as a recruitment consultant, I see it all. But the most impressive interviewees are those who have real passion and spark. They've done their research but they're not boring you with it or asking you lots of questions. They want the job – they tell you as much. Their answers are short and to the point, and they look me in the eye when they're telling me. My pet hate is fidgeters – I don't trust applicants who can't sit still. If you get nervous, sit on your hands or hold a copy of your CV to stop the wriggling. ❞

How to be impressive on the phone

Whether you're doing a phone interview, a conference call or cold-calling a company you'd love to work for, a good telephone manner is essential. Try the following:

◆ Smile – you can hear it in your voice.

◆ Keep a pen, paper and calculator to hand in case you need them.

◆ Don't smoke, chew or slurp – those sounds travel.

◆ If you stand up your voice sounds stronger and more authoritative.

- ◆ Pace the call, don't rush and let the other person speak.

- ◆ Avoid 'er', 'um', 'huh', and the rest – they'll make you sound dumb.

Expensive tastes

Networking doesn't come cheap. When you are pursuing someone for a job, a promotion or a contract, you have to be prepared to spend the cash. People like to be wined and dined. Or a gift received at a desk on a dull day will always make you a special person in someone's mind. If you're working on behalf of your company, you should be able to claim for such expenses. Ask what the policy is when you start (not in the interview – it will make you look a bit flash and money-hungry). Keep all receipts in a folder and try to make a date to fill out a form once a month. They do add up and they do get lost. Take them home and file them while you're watching television one night. If you can't claim things through work, because your expenses are purely self-promoting and personal, think of filing them, too – to the taxman. If they really are necessary in your career you may get a rebate so investigate. Don't wine and dine so much that you are forced to eat gruel every other night of the week. Spend within your limits.

Asking for a pay rise

How can you delicately ask for a pay rise? It's difficult – believe you me, I'd rather ask for my boss's bra size than for a few measly thousands. But the sad truth is that if you don't ask, you don't get! Average yearly pay rises only amount to about 3 per cent of your basic salary, so if you want to buy a house or build up your Jimmy Choo collection, you're going to have to bite the bullet and take a long walk to your manager's door.

Here are ten tips to help you get out those five difficult words: 'I deserve a pay rise':

1. Find out how much you are worth. Ask around. Get an idea from jobs advertised, from your colleagues and your contemporaries in other companies. Are you underpaid for your role? This will help you decide – and by how much!

2. Be confident, don't stress out. I know, as a manager of over 40 people, that it is cheaper to keep the brave little blighter who asked for a small increase than to recruit and train a new person. All sensible employers know this. Only be worried if you've been slacking off lately – your 'pay rise or I resign' speech could backfire and give your boss an easy exit.

3. Increase your value in the months leading up to your demand by working harder and better. Network across departments, socialise with your boss, and volunteer to help on extra things – even if it means giving up a few weekends or evenings.

4. Keep learning and pushing yourself. You'll never feel bad about asking for a pay increase if you're taking time out to study and get extra qualifications.

5. When asking for more cash, don't be aggressive. Be assertive instead. Don't threaten or moan. I always say you should prove you deserve more because of your merits, not because of other people's failings.

6. While you're being assertive, set some limits. How long has your boss got to think about it, what are your other options, how much do you want? Always ask for a certain amount – not just a general rise, and ask for a response within two weeks.

7. Second-guess your boss. What objections is he or she going to raise? Anticipate the problems and come straight back at them with a legitimate answer. Be careful about being too pushy though. Some things to do with finances and budget will be out of your direct superior's hands and you must respect that.

8. Argue for a rise on the basis of your performance – don't say your boyfriend earns more than you and it's making you feel inadequate. And don't say your mortgage is too huge or your credit card bill needs paying off. Irrelevant! All that matters is what you do at work and what you should be making for your labour.

9. Always make notes about the things you have achieved and added to the company, list all your accomplishments and all the times you've worked outside and beyond your current job description. Bring all the documents to the meeting for back-up.

10. If you're not getting anywhere with a straightforward pay rise, negotiate for better hours, benefits and perks. Training and a travel card keeps my staff happy during tough financial times when I can't offer them the pay rises I'd like to.

HEIDI, 38

❝ As a manager, every year I am given a certain sum that I can distribute to my team as pay rises. It's an awful challenge – more often than not I wish I could give them all something impressive. But I have to judge who deserves it most on three things: attitude, skills and pushing themselves to be irreplaceable. Some people are good, some people are very good – while others go out of their way to help their colleagues, think of new ideas, offer solutions and put in extra hours in times of emergency. They get the money! ❞

How to be a cool colleague

You probably spend more time with your colleagues than your loved ones. It sucks, right? Well make your life a little easier by not being the office bore/bitch/jerk or loser by working on your office etiquette. There's no point networking brilliantly with external clients if your internal colleagues hate you!

1. Don't steal other people's things. Yes, we all like to borrow a stapler or mug every now and again, but return it. Nothing is more infuriating – however minor it seems.

2. Treat the workplace as you would your home. Don't leave a mess in communal areas. Keep the kitchen and the bathrooms fragrant and hygienic.

3. Don't shout, scream, attack or physically assault colleagues – however annoying they are. Believe me, I've

wanted to put someone's head through a wall before but I took the upper ground. He looked like a pathetic little bully, I looked down my nose at him without screaming at him to stop lying. It worked; I got the upper hand by acting intelligently. Dignity, always dignity.

4. However useful and wonderful the telephone and email systems are at your place, get off your arse and talk face to face occasionally. It makes for better rapport – and will stop your eyes going funny from staring at a computer screen all day long.

5. Be trustworthy. If you are told a secret once and you share it, don't ever expect to be trusted again.

6. Don't expect your colleagues to carry your workload. The working week ends on Friday afternoon – not Thursday lunchtime.

7. Always contribute to the pub whip-round or someone's leaving collection. You have to be very mean to resent chucking in a few pounds.

8. Remember, if you're gossiping and backstabbing someone, that person will assume you are doing it about them, too. No one likes nastiness – unless they're nasty themselves. Bitch to a friend over a beer after work. In the office, be kind, considerate and keep your nose clean.

9. Don't be a total arse-licker, your co-workers will find you fake and irritating.

10. Acknowledge other people's successes with good grace and good humour.

Secrets of Success

◆ Work is important, but don't let it take over your life. If you spend all day in the office, then all night networking with contacts, you might suddenly wake up at 60 and think, 'Bugger!'

◆ Keep your CV updated and saved at home in case you have to leave your office suddenly ... and never go back.

◆ Avoid smiling gormlessly or gazing off into the distance in job interviews or meetings. It's very unbecoming for a modern girl.

◆ If you haven't heard anything two weeks after a job interview, send a polite follow-up email or letter asking if a decision has been made.

◆ Don't panic about starting at the bottom of the ladder. If you're someone's assistant, don't get bitter – get ahead! Everyone has to start somewhere. And conversely, never be rude to an assistant – they could be your boss one day.

◆ You can't love all the people all the time. Avoid the people who make your skin crawl. You don't need to be friends with them, just be civil. Anything to avoid a public brawl – which even if it's their fault, will reflect badly on both of you!

◆ Treat your team well ... but don't let them take the piss.

◆ Don't get drunk and spill the beans at your leaving do. You never know who you will be working with – or for – again. And if times change, you may even want to go back to the same company. So wave goodbye with a smile and no slagging off. Fate has a funny way of bringing people together again.

Chapter Nine

The art of
communication

WHETHER YOU'RE GOSSIPING about the new mayor with your neighbours or sending an important letter to the financial director of your dream company, communication is the key to successful networking. You need to listen and you need to be heard. You need to know the right way to write, and the wrong way to read into things.

You got mail

Is email the most fabulous invention in the world? A database, diary, social planner, fax machine and post box in one – hoorah! And now with BlackBerries you can be in constant email contact, which has its good and bad sides. Good: you can reference back to check plans and leave an unobtrusive message rather than call. Bad: you can feel your office following you around your home, hotel, relationship – I've even got RSI from my 'Crackberry' addiction.

With all this in mind, here are some email etiquette tips to avoid communication confusion:

◆ Emails are there to save time, so don't write a business email like you would a letter. You don't need to add the date, your address or a formal greeting. Be polite, brief and to the point.

◆ Reference emails clearly in the subject box. This will help you and the recipient to find it quickly and store it carefully. Update the title if the same email is being sent backwards and forwards, or forwarded to someone else.

◆ Capitals can be rude out of context – you may mean to emphasise a point, but sensitive people will think you're angry, shouting or impatient. Only go upper case one word at a time for dramatic impact or in the subject box.

◆ Don't try to be too funny, and certainly try not to incorporate sarcasm into your mail – it's impossible in type.

◆ Try not to write more than one screen of text. People are busy at work and emails should be used precisely – your colleagues may only have time to skim-read for major points.

◆ Avoid forwarding those dull chain letters or competitions. They don't work, or don't open. Why bother? Circulators are the bane of a busy person's life.

◆ Don't expect to receive a reply straight away. Just because you work long hours and then spend the 12 hours out of the office checking your emails at home, not everyone is the same. Send an email with enough time for a reply within your deadline.

◆ Don't defuse a major war with an email – be brave and face off your enemy or the troublemaker in person. It'll be solved sooner and off the record. If you suspect you've received an annoying, non-urgent email, don't open it until you're back on the clock. Don't let a nasty message ruin your weekend.

◆ Blind copying should be used rarely. It's unfair for a third person to be unknowingly in on a private email chat, unless you or your boss feels it is necessary to cover yourselves.

◆ Don't write anything on email you wouldn't want your boss to see – or your mother! These things have a habit of leaking.

RUTH, 30

❝ I had a few months of receiving the nastiest emails from a man at work – not my boss, but another senior manager. They were full of unnecessary spite and random accusations. I showed them to my boss, who advised me to store them in a private email account, and she told me that he'd been sending them to lots of people and she had received many complaints. She let the director know and he was disciplined. Email insults are just as powerful as the spoken word, and this man was a cowardly bully to think he could get away with it. ❞

Your auto signature

Make sure you have a sensible sign-off – a signature that is suitable for all recipients, from your mum to your clients. No 'See ya, chica!' or 'Later dude', and even the ever so arse-licking 'Yours respectfully' is a bit much. I'd recommend just doing the basics: your name, title, address, email address and a phone and fax number. You can then add your own farewell message relevant to each email, whether it be 'Best regards' or 'Lots of love'.

Easy access

Email has opened up the world of networking like nothing else – giving out a number is a risk and calling someone is a brave step. Email eliminates this. If you are relying on email as your chief correspondence tool, then make sure your email server is working and reliable, that you check it regularly, and reply regularly, and that your email name is sensible. If you get a lot of private emails and are worried about the company computer geek discovering your inner-most thoughts, set up a private account.

NB Be careful of what you write and how you write it because the tone of an email can easily be misinterpreted. Other email issues include (a) if it breaks you're buggered so back up everything, and print important things out; and (b) you can get a big bottom – you start emailing people ten feet away rather than getting up and going for a one-on-one.

Saved by the bell

Not everything can be done over email – in fact some things are better said. Strangely though, picking up the phone does scare people. You wouldn't believe the number of my team who have to be cajoled into it. 'Have you been in touch?'

'I've emailed.'

'Try picking up the phone?' Five minutes later, they've emerged from their moment of fear and resistance with an answer. Amazing that.

A good telephone manner is an essential skill in the modern world, whether responding to an angry call from your boss or a prospective date. Here are some tips:

◆ Never assume the person on the other end of the line knows who you are; introduce yourself and give your reason for calling.

◆ Speak clearly and if there's an awkward pause say, 'What can I do for you?' (if you're returning their call), or 'The reason I'm calling is ...' (if you're calling out of the blue).

◆ Don't assume the person you're calling is free to chat. Ask if it's OK, and try to round up any chat (unless with a close friend) after 15 minutes.

◆ Keep your calling to decent times – office hours are best, and never before 8.00 a.m. or after 10.00 p.m. unless it's an absolute emergency. Don't call people on their mobiles if you know they are out of the country unless it's an absolute must – they will have to pay the (extortionate) price.

◆ Don't keep a phone stuck to your ear during social engagements. It's rude and will make whoever you're with feel like second best.

On message

Your answering machine message gives people an immediate insight into your psyche. So record it carefully. Joke messages or music gets very repetitive very quickly, so stick to your normal voice stating clear instructions for leaving a message. Be brief and professional. Don't leave your address or your mobile number on the message.

Try: 'Please leave your name, number and reason for calling and I'll get back to you as soon as possible.'

Don't try: 'Hi there, crazy kids. Tell me who you are and I'll call back if I can be bothered!'

When it comes to leaving a message there are a few more rules that apply:

1. Don't be nervous of the bleeps. If you are worried, hang up and start again – don't leave a series of 'um's and 'ah's.

2. Keep your message brief – you don't want to be cut off mid-sentence.

3. Keep to the point – if everything else escapes you just leave your name and number.

4. Don't leave a rude or personal message – you don't know who will get to it first.

5. Messages do get lost and garbled. Don't get paranoid that your new networking friend has ignored you. Leave it for 24 hours then try again.

6. On the other hand, don't phone-stalk. Do not fill up someone's message box with your needy messages.

7. Don't lie about where you are in a message, in case a sound in the background gives you away.

8. Before leaving an important voicemail, practise message etiquette by leaving one for yourself on your own answering machine. Listen out for speed, accent and tone.

9. Leaving messages can be good if you want to remind someone of something gently without talking to them. Leave a message while they are at work, flying, and so on.

10. While we're talking about message etiquette, always note down your own messages carefully and pass them on if necessary.

Mobile madness

What is it about modern girls – if we're not on our mobiles, were checking them, buying ring tones for them or updating them? We're obsessed. But remember, ladies, they are no longer unique or a novelty, so keep the noise down. If you're in a busy place, keep calls brief and quiet – the whole train carriage isn't interested in your dinner plans. Also pay attention to the ring tone and volume – some are far more irritating than others, and can make you look very immature if your phone starts ringing in a meeting.

So when should you use your mobile? In a genuine emergency, when on your own, or when quickly making or confirming plans.

When should you answer someone else's phone? Use the same rule as if you were in their home – would you pick up the receiver then? Probably not. If they were expecting an urgent call they'd have probably taken their phone with them. The great thing about mobiles is that they record numbers and messages. Leave it.

Texting is another benefit of mobiles – they are quick, easy and cheap to send. They can be ignored until you are ready to respond. But really use this method of communicating for your friends and family only. Texting new networking contacts seems a bit flirty and familiar. And over-texters do have a reputation as being a bit dumb. Come on, you've seen those groups of girls in bars who don't talk, just text, like they're being hypnotised by the phone screen. Texting, again, is for quick and simple messages, not for all night chit-chat. Unless you're on the pull.

The lost art of letter writing

People seem to be too stressed or busy to sit down and write a proper letter these days, but sometimes it's correct and really does make a good impression. Don't send a letter to do the following: sack someone, make someone redundant, cancel a date, end a relationship or announce you're pregnant – these things are all better received in person. But do send a letter in these circumstances:

- ◆ A covering letter attached to your CV is a must. More on this in Chapter 8.

- ◆ Thank-you letters show you've taken time and effort and are genuinely grateful.

- ◆ Birthday cards must be sent in the post, not via email.

- ◆ Formal invitations should be thought about and posted, not using an all-round text.

- ◆ Special or difficult occasions deserve a letter or a 'with sympathy' or 'get well soon' card. News and views in a handwritten letter will always be warmly received and it shows a lot of thought and care.

CATHERINE, 33

6 It really annoys me when people don't send thank-you letters within a month of an event or a present – I think it's the easiest way to show modern manners still exist. On the other hand, it really stands out when someone is a good letter writer. As a recruitment consultant, I hold a lot of opportunities in my hand for other people, and I can't help being impressed, and therefore biased towards, the people who write to thank me for my time and help. 9

Don't be nosy

No matter how tempting it is, never open someone else's mail. Yes, your business rival is away on holiday and you've got the chance to go through her post and sift through her leads – but you will probably be picked up on the CCTV. And don't open a friend or partner's post either. Just because you share everything else with your partner, you don't need to share all the details of his bank account, and so on. I've had some friends who have got too nosy and really ruined some great things – from surprise birthday parties to engagements. Hands off.

Happy talk

Silence is golden? With a hangover, maybe, but in networking situations what you have to say for yourself will distinguish you from the crowd. There's no quicker way for making contacts, gaining respect and getting things done your way. But remember: it's quality not quantity that counts, so don't let your mouth run away with you.

Small talk, big impression

Sometimes it's a struggle to go out there and make chit-chat with strangers. If you're even a little bit tired, pre-menstrual or stressed, it sometimes seems better to stay in with a muzzle than to go out and try to sweet-talk the world. Work events can be a great opportunity to talk to your boss about how wonderful you are or to bond with your team, but it can be a very long night if you are stuck schmoozing boring clients or colleagues determined to talk shop.

The hardest thing to do is start a conversation – so just remember: people like to talk about themselves and recent news (be it the weather or so-and-so's promotion). If you go to any social gathering with a moderately nosy nature and a new celebrity story, you'll be fine. Buy a newspaper or two before a big networking event so that you can join a conversation with an interesting fact, or at the very least know what is going on in the discussion around you. Hot (safe) topics include:

◆ **Physical attributes:** 'Is that a new haircut/new dress/are those cool shoes new?

◆ **The venue:** 'Have you been here before, do you know where the bar is …?'

◆ **The weather:** 'Oh, I had trouble getting here in this rain this evening!'

◆ **The host:** 'How do you know Jonny? We went to school together …'

◆ **Your job:** 'I'm here as part of my new role as [fill in the blank].'

◆ **Their job:** ask about their career path, job satisfaction, and so on.

Or, you can always try the simple route: 'Hi, I'm Ms Fabulous, how are you?' And don't be afraid to add that you don't know anyone else and are feeling a little shy and alone. Most kind-hearted people will take you under their wing straight away. Go in search of someone who also appears to be on their lonesome-ownsome. At a party, position yourself by the buffet table or bar to catch waifs and strays. Don't linger around the loos though, you'll look like a perv! But do run to a cubicle on your own for a quick breather if you've been socialising and small-talking your sassy arse off and you need to escape a very boring new acquaintance.

Small talk can be tricky, as you don't want to go into your life history but you don't want to appear aloof either. It means sometimes being superficial, but it can help you to establish (a) who's who; (b) who to avoid; and (c) who to talk to next.

When having this introductory chit-chat, don't dominate the conversation, always listen and don't jump to conclusions.

Avoid the following subjects at all costs: politics, religion, salaries, divorces, plastic surgery, drastic weight loss, and how bad your boss/company/colleagues are. You'll bore, scare or insult someone – and at the small-talking stage you don't know how important they are going to be to you.

Once you feel comfortable, and you think you should develop your relationship with the new person you're talking to, move from chit-chat to meaningful conversation. But still be careful. Don't say too much – especially to your boss's wife, for example. Everything you say will get straight back. Observe your audience; if they start to twitch nervously, shut up. Refrain from emotional subjects if there's something you haven't got a handle on yet (your recent divorce, your mother's death, your redundancy). If someone asks you a personal question that you're not ready to answer yet, don't get pushed into it. Politely state that you don't wish to talk about it, thank you. 'Oh don't ask! I'll get us a refill!' is a good alternative. This rule should also apply if a subject comes up that you have an extreme opinion on. It's better to withdraw than to risk a full-on clash.

KATIE, 30

❝ I attended a wedding far too soon after the breakdown of my own marriage. I had to attend – it was a good friend's special day – but rather than treating me with kid gloves (as I'd kind of expected from old friends), half of them asked me personal details and gave me their own firm views about how sensible I was or what a mistake I was making, whereas the other half ignored me until they were drunk enough to tell me all their own relationship woes. No one knows what truly goes on in a relationship except the two people in it, and I let these people verbally assault me when I should have walked away. ❞

Social circles

You have to keep circulating if you want to become an expert networker. It's not enough to stick to the side of someone you have enjoyed meeting, or hanging out in a familiar circle. Keep moving and introducing yourself. Don't shark the room or follow people – you'll look desperate and hard-nosed. No, rather than sharking, glide around the main areas of an event or party, spend a little longer with the good, interesting people, step away from the losers and ask the host who you really should be talking to. When I have to go to an event for work – but can't wait to go home or meet friends – I always follow the same formula. I'll check in my coat and bag at the cloakroom so it's not obvious I'm only staying for a short while and I make my way to say hello to the people I know (I try to remember a few relevant details about business contacts so I can have a quick, friendly chat, such as the names of their kids, their recent holiday). There's no point in wasting time at the buffet or bar, so I avoid those, and escape as soon as I've scoped the room and made sure I wasn't missing anyone. Easy-peasy.

Compliments shcompliments!

Don't go overboard with the compliments. Yeah, we all like to be flattered, but screaming, 'I LOVE your skirt! Love it! Love it!' at someone you've just met may be a bit over the top. And be careful with the compliments you give (no reference to successful plastic surgery or your conversation partner finally being able to control their kids, please) – and don't comment on people's weight loss, however kindly you mean it. You're bound to get the pounds dropped, or diminished dress size, wrong, and therefore leave the person feeling as if they used to look like a beached whale!

NB if someone gives you a compliment, accept it graciously and say thank you – and move on. Don't wallow in your own fabulousness, or reject the other person's kindness. It sounds fake anyway, if you mutter, 'What this old thing? Found it on the floor,' and so on, when you're clearly in top-to-toe Prada.

Troubling talk

If you can't think of anything to say … try the aforementioned topics, or if you can't say anything nice don't say anything at all. Leave it up to the other person. Conversation is a two-way thing and if you've made an effort but they're not playing ball, the onus is on them.

If you can't escape a chatterbox, don't yawn or run away. Subtly look around to grab someone to join you. If you can't see any victims, say forcefully, 'It's been nice talking to you, I should now go and mingle,' and turn towards someone new quickly.

If you've got a case of the motor mouth, when you're networking try not to cover too much ground or oversell yourself, which are common mistakes to make. It comes from our natural instinct to fill silence, and to make people like us. But slow down, take a breather and ask for someone else's views.

If you can't escape a pervert – such as you're asking a guy old enough to be your dad for advice about what course you should take, but he misinterprets this as a come-on – as soon as he makes the first suggestive comment, halt any further embarrassment for both of you by excusing yourself to the loo (he can't follow you there). If it really gets too bad and you don't have friends with you to bat him away, leave. You won't enjoy spending the evening hiding behind the curtains.

If you say something really mortifying, apologise immediately, backtrack if you can without looking too silly, and then don't let it eat you up. Alcohol is normally involved and the good news is: that means everyone else may be tiddly, too, and not remember. If the next day you are still worried about it, email or call with an official apology to all those you think you offended. Then really and truly, forget about it. If people tease you in the future, take it with good grace and a 'yeah, whatever' attitude.

Talking in public

Cringe – public speaking is terrifying! Standing up in front of a sea of faces and trying to get your point across is difficult and intimidating. But as you keep networking and climbing the corporate ladder, you'll be expected to overcome your fear and get on with it. I've had to give a few talks to rooms of over 400 people. I've hated it, but survived, and here's how:

1. Be prepared. Get to know the room, check the microphone is working, and so on.

2. Use cards and your imagination to talk, for sure, but do have the full speech written down and with you in case of emergencies.

3. Keep eye contact with a friendly (familiar if possible) face at the front. It'll steady your nerves and stop you feeling dizzy … and from taking in just how many people are staring at you.

4. Don't try to be too funny. If a joke falls flat, you'll feel it.

5. If you blush or stumble over your words, who cares. Could anyone else do any better?

6. Make it personal if possible, at least chuck in a few relevant anecdotes. It'll make it easier to remember.

7. Keep it short and make it relevant – the fewer tangents the better.

8. Slow it down – you may want to get off stage but people want to hear you.

9. Don't shock or be politically incorrect.

10. Remember: it's a big deal to you, but not such a big deal to anyone else. Don't stress too much, everyone else will be thinking how brave you are!

Is all PR good PR?

Believe you me, not all PR is good PR! In my current job, the New York newspapers report every week that I've dramatically marched out or I've been humiliatingly fired (or worse!). It's never true, but apparently it's interesting to someone. These days modern girls need to be aware that they can't always run their own public relations machine, and modern networking isn't just about how you choose to communicate with others, but what the media wishes to communicate about you. If your job is leading you to become a public persona or a figurehead in your industry, it might be wise to take some media training. These experts can advise you on everything from what to wear on television to what not to say during a radio interview. If your budget doesn't run to specific training, seek out your company's press officer – or, at the very least, marketing director, and badger the other people in your office who have dealings with the press for much-needed info. Here are a few tips:

◆ The key thing to remember is not to be forced or tricked into saying something you shouldn't. Think before you speak. Never repeat a question, as this could be used as your soundbite even though they're not your words.

◆ Avoid umming and aahing too much in any kind of interview – television or print – as it makes you look stupid.

◆ Don't try to be funny or sarcastic, it doesn't translate in interviews and can be misconstrued.

◆ Listen to the questions carefully. If you don't know something, don't make it up – ask for a few moments, or say 'I can't comment on that, I'm sorry.'

◆ Before you do any interview with the press, check that it is fine with your superior. Your company could have a no-quote policy.

◆ Keep a few decent pictures of you on file in case you are required to send one to a publication for print. You don't want to have to hurriedly get a friend to take one in the office – you could be having a bad hair day.

◆ If you're going on television, wear something plain, avoid patterns and loud colours, and get your make-up done if you can (shiny skin and dark circles always look worse under bright lights).

◆ Be careful, but do try to enjoy it – think of how proud you're making your mum … and remember, it really is only tomorrow's fish and chip wrapper!

NB If you're at the forefront of a barrage of personally nasty or professionally damaging reports, there are a few things you can do. First, make your boss aware, and your human resources manager if appropriate. If you don't have an in-house legal department, think of finding a lawyer to ask their advice on whether you should pursue it in the courts. If you want to go a different route, call the journalist for an 'off the record' chat and advise him of his mistakes. They won't print an apology (journalists hate that!) but they should think twice about doing it again.

Secrets of Success

◆ Listen more than you talk when meeting new, impressive people you wish to network with. You don't know what you could learn from them, and by listening rather than talking you can avoid unleashing any faux pas.

◆ Always start a letter, email or a phone call with a sincere, 'How are you?' Manners cost nothing, remember.

◆ Beware of speakerphones – you don't know who is listening.

◆ Stalking via email or phone is still stalking.

◆ Every modern girl should keep an up-to-date phone number, email and address list. This will save you lots of time – it's always the detail you haven't got that you need.

◆ Check your messages regularly and reply asap – even if it's just a phone call or email saying, 'The full answer needs more research but I wanted you to know I'm on it.'

◆ Faxing or mailing correspondence forces you to be more careful, so address formal or legal matters this way.

◆ If a new person you're trying to schmooze hasn't replied to your third message, it's time to forget about them. They aren't interested.

◆ If your phone rings during an interview or meeting, or while someone is talking at a conference, turn it off immediately and apologise quietly if necessary. You should be ashamed for not turning it off in the first place!

◆ When talking to new people, speak slowly and clearly. Really, train yourself in front of a mirror or record yourself if you need the practice. Fast, mumbled, gabbled speech makes the person you're talking to feel uncomfortable.

◆ Use a person's name in conversation – it shows you've remembered and are focusing on them.

◆ First impressions make the lasting impression ... and we cynical humans give only 30 seconds to form an opinion of people. But give your fellow networkers a few minutes longer. You don't know who you'll miss – and they might just be nervous.

◆ Don't offer your business card as you shake someone's hand. It's nicer to give them out at the end, and looks less pushy or that you give them to everyone. Being given your business card should seem like an honour.

◆ Earwigging is a curse for all we women – just don't admit what you were doing by butting into a conversation and then correcting the chatterers.

◆ Don't interview someone out of context. Ask questions, let them answer, but then share something of yourself. The conversation shouldn't be a one-way thing or an interrogation.

◆ While out networking socially, include newcomers with an open mind. If you're having a chat in a group, and a new person joins, fill them in on what you were discussing and include them.

◆ The best way to have something interesting to talk about is to do something worth talking about! Get away from your networking frenzy to travel, read, listen to new albums, get to the cinema and take up a hobby. Yes, you have got the time, missy!

Chapter Ten

Dating direction

ALL WORK AND NO PLAY MAKES you a dull modern woman. Let's face it, it's a toss-up for most of us twenty-first-century girls: which is more important, having the perfect relationship or having the perfect career? Can you have both? Can one help the other? Your friends and family are a constant, a given ... but love takes up as much work as, well, work!

How can networking help your dating?

The more confident and content you are in other areas of your life, the more your self-assurance and happiness will grow in the romantic arena. People who are doing a job they love, that they're good at and that they are respected for will have more of those qualities to put into a relationship. I also find it's the highly efficient doers in life that manage to spin all the plates of life without over-analysing or panicking about one thing.

If you're in a serious relationship, your man should give you the space and support to really launch yourself into your career. Having a strong, secure relationship is very important and will help you cope with the stress and office politics. Working until 9.00 p.m. every night for a week won't be so sad if your boyfriend is at home, running you a bath and cooking you supper. Use your strong relationship as a sounding board: it allows you to bounce ideas off it, gives you energy and allows you to take chances and risks that perhaps you wouldn't do if you were on your own and feeling vulnerable.

But remember, you need to support your man, too. It's not all about you (and your boss, and your promotion, and your salary ...), you need to share your experiences, time and patience with him. Don't put your career on the back burner for his benefit – but certainly be there during the tough times. Meet his new team if he asks you to, however dull it sounds. Don't invite your girlfriends round if he needs a quiet night in to prepare a report. If he's really tied up for a few months in the office, don't moan that he won't take a beach holiday with you. Take a friend instead!

If you're single, networking can be a great way to meet new eligible men. You're out and about and looking fabulous, inspired to make small talk and confident that you're up to date with the latest news and have sparkling views.

Can you be passionate and professional?

The following tips and advice are useful for all areas of your romantic life – and any kind of date. However, as a modern girl with a career in progress, you need to make sure that your dating shenanigans do not negatively impact on your office reputation. Yes, love is blind and often encourages all good sense to fly out of the window. But do try to keep level-headed when the worlds of romance and work combine.

How to flirt at work events

The key is not to be too obvious (especially if your CEO is in attendance) and don't forget why you're there – meeting someone sexy is a great perk, but you're there to work and make contacts for every area of your life ... not just in the bedroom. Outrageous flirting may put other women off you. No decent girl likes a man's woman. Make sure you can focus on the interesting woman's conversation without your tongue hanging out whenever the cute guy from your marketing department walks past!

Stay focused, but flirt by:

◆ **Being yourself.** If you are talking to a fanciable male don't suddenly put on another persona that your boss might question later that evening. Stay true, don't exaggerate your position and don't make up any white lies that your colleagues could pick up on.

◆ **Wearing a fabulous outfit.** No tits 'n' arse – you're more sophisticated than that. Try a coquettishly fabulous outfit, a well-fitting suit or a dress that clings to your curves. Make sure your hair, make-up and nails are immaculate. Men appreciate these little touches.

◆ **Asking a trusted colleague for help,** a married friend would be perfect. You can't spend your whole evening sharking for men, split the chore with the chosen friend to allow you to focus on business networking. Get her to report back once an hour with any hot spots.

◆ **Be sociable in general** – don't just talk and flirt with the guy you fancy, go up to his group and make a few jokes, offer to get the drinks in ... then just catch his eye and hold his gaze for a few seconds longer than necessary, mimic his body language and position, subtly twist your hair or stroke your neck. These little things will make him aware that you're a sensual woman, who might have a soft spot for him, but there's nothing so obvious that your boss will be embarrassed or you'll be thought of as acting inappropriately.

Jo, 36

❝ I met my husband at a banking seminar in London. Yes, I know it's not the most romantic of meeting places but there was something about the way he looked in his suit and how he asked interesting questions during the open discussion. I made sure I sat next to him during the afternoon lecture, and then bonded with him over a shared love of Hong Kong and an ambition to transfer there with our respective companies. He saw instantly that I was the female version of him, he's told me since. We swapped cards, supposedly for work reasons, but we both knew more would happen. ❞

A networker's flirty conversation starters

If you see a hot guy at a work or committee event, try a few simple ice-breakers:

- ◆ 'Do you know where the cloakroom is?'

- ◆ 'You don't happen to have a taxi firm's number do you?'

- ◆ 'Have I seen you before?'

- ◆ 'I really recognise the host's name – tell me more.'

- ◆ 'Did I leave my drink over here?'

- ◆ 'My friend used to work for your firm …'

- ◆ 'Does the DJ take requests/what time does the entertainment start?'

- ◆ 'I've just been for a manicure; can you grab my card from my pocket?'

◆ 'Leaving now? Too bad – I wanted to ask you what you thought of ...'

◆ 'I've had a rough day in the office. How do you unwind?'

The save-time test

When you're at a networking event, you can't just hunt for single men. You need to spend time talking to contacts and clients, too. Here is a 30-minute checklist to keep in mind – and to stop you wasting time on the wrong kind of man. It's amazing what you can find out about a man in only half an hour, in public!

Use your light-hearted banter to deduce if he's single; is he more interested in you than himself? (He doesn't look in the mirror at his reflection over your head – bravo!) Is he able to hold a conversation? Do you have a similar sense of humour and do you approve of his dress sense? Ticks for the above all mean he's worth pursuing. Don't ask him for his opinion on marriage and children in this 30-minute 'getting to know you' chat.

How to swap details

The business card is a perfect tool for the nervy flirter – it doesn't look too serious or sexy, and it has your email on it (the perfect method of communicating for anxious daters). Always keep them in your purse. Don't scrawl your number on his tie in lipstick. If you work near each other, suggest a lunch date equidistant to your offices. If you work together, suggest a drink after work – but not in the usual after-work hangout of your colleagues (they'll interfere).

If he asks for your details, stay calm. Don't clap or cry or jump up and down. A simple, 'Of course, it would be nice to meet up,' and if you don't have a business card handy an elegantly scribbled name and number on a napkin will suffice. If you are worried about what to say, when he calls for the first time, let your answering machine pick up.

If you're both too shy to swap details, make sure you get a run down of his social calendar – so you can accidentally-on-purpose cross paths in the coffee shop or bump into him at his gym. Don't stalk, but adapt your routine to open up opportunities.

The sensible networker's overnight pack

If you meet someone at a party and decide to go back for the night, or if you have started a relationship and are spending more time at your boyfriend's flat, you're going to need to take emergency precautions. It's all about keeping up appearances, so keep the following in your handbag (or in your desk drawer at the very least): bronzing powder; mascara; tights or stockings; clean knickers; mouth freshener or toothbrush; condoms; mobile phone and cash – in case you need to get a taxi from the back of beyond to make it to work on time the morning after the night before.

E-male etiquette

Flirting via email at work can really help a dull day go quickly, but be careful – your work emails can be monitored and viewed by the company. Don't even think about using swear words or sending porn. These are sackable offences. Be funny but not too wacky or ironic – it doesn't translate well. Send one email; don't send 20. Wait for a reply. And don't get grumpy if he doesn't reply immediately. I have a real attitude if emails aren't returned straight away – because I have a BlackBerry, I'm on them in minutes. But not everyone has access to a computer at home or while travelling, so chill out. Don't be overbearing before you've even gone on your first date.

Flirting at other people's work events

This is networking of a different sort. You need to think about your friend's reputation as much as your own. You may be there to flirt but she invited you over all the other modern girls because you're fun, intelligent and sociable. Prove it. That said, other people's work dos are a great way to meet new men – for a start, you know he's gainfully employed and going places, and has the money to take you out. But stay clear of anyone she fancies – and her boss. That would put her in an impossible position. Ask her to point you in the direction of the company's most eligible bachelor – one she doesn't fancy and who is single. Bond by talking about your friend and the company (do a little investigating beforehand).

NB If you spend too much time flirting at work events or having dangerous liaisons at company parties you'll exhaust yourself – and the place where this will show up the most is at work. If you're needing an intravenous drip of coffee to get you through the morning meeting, you know

---

your social life is taking too much strain on your overall well-being. Forget about romance and refocus by going booze-free for a month, having a few early nights and getting away for a while to get out of your dating routine.

Love-work balance

The most stressful, time-consuming episode in a relationship is the beginning – when you're tempted to have 'stay in bed' days, or to leave work early to meet him in the pub. You can waste hours in the office daydreaming, doodling and emailing. This is the time you have to be strong and focused. If you've got an important meeting or work trip coming up, you have to prepare and plan properly – and your mind has to be on the job. Keep the girlishness to nights out with your friends; keep the office for working. If you must gossip about your new man, do it when your boss is out of the office.

When your relationship develops more, and you're used to all of his romantic benefits, you'll be able to concentrate on work more. This is the time to make sure your home life away from the office is as calm and stress-free as possible – to allow you to take on extra work and pressure, to build your career and your reputation.

Men to avoid

Your relationship should make you feel valued, adored and protected. These are key things to take into your career with you. A relationship that gives you the stability to shine is vital. Some men sap you of your power rather than lift your spirits. You will not get the support and comfort you need from one of the following ten types of man. Avoid at all costs:

1. The jealous lover – you're more successful than him? He hates you.

2. The lazy lover – he can't be bothered, your motivation dips.

3. The vain lover – the more he loves himself, the more insecure you'll feel.

4. The party lover – he wants you out drinking every night, not in the office by 9.00 a.m.

5. The chauvinistic lover – 'Don't work, honey, just get pregnant.'

6. The angry lover – nothing you do is right, you'll become a nervous wreck.

7. The hippie lover – he doesn't want you to work for your boss, money, the company…

8. The competitive lover – he'll put you down and enjoy your failures.

9. The lecherous lover – you won't be able to take him anywhere with you.

10. The lying lover – you'll spend so long wondering where he is, you won't be able to concentrate on work and impressing your boss.

JANE, 35

❝ In my twenties, I foolishly married a man who felt he was in competition with me. Every time I got a pay rise, he'd bitch and moan and resent it, even though it meant I could spend more on the house and holidays for the pair of us. Eventually, it broke us up. I couldn't stand the jealousy and viciousness – especially when he was made redundant. Now, I'm married again and my new partner is supportive and encouraging. He persuades me to be tougher at work and to constantly rethink ideas. Because of him, I feel happier and more sure of myself, and my design business has flourished. The best thing: he happily lets me pay for dinner when I win a new contract without trying to put me down in the car on the way back to reclaim his penis! ❞

Office romances

So you've fallen for a guy at work – who hasn't? But it's how you handle it (and how he handles you) that makes the difference! This could be the trickiest piece of networking of your life. You need to remain professional and unbiased while your head is in the clouds. And then of course, you need to remain diplomatic and fair if it all collapses. Good luck!

Dating a colleague

Over 50 per cent of adults in Britain meet their partner in the workplace. Think about it, you spend so much time there, it's bound to happen. Your eyes meet across the photocopier, he cheekily asks to borrow your stapler, and you keep bumping into each other at the water cooler. Things can get pretty hot and steamy between those grey, office walls. But you have to think about each other's reputations – as well as the stomachs of your colleagues. Don't go for a full-on snog in the office, even if you think the coast is clear and you can get away with it. A quick kiss will suffice. And don't go round groping each other either, it's most unpleasant for those observing the scene – especially when they have to take a conference call with you later in the day. You can't stand around and flirt and giggle all day, or plan what you're having for dinner. If you want to communicate about romantic or non-work related things, do so via email (or if it's of a more private nature, by text). Try not to just talk about work. If you're travelling home together, make it a rule that you discuss office politics for the journey, and then change the subject the minute you reach the front door. Tell your direct superiors about your relationship if you feel you should, but don't partake in general, reckless gossip. Loose talking costs jobs.

Dating your boss

How interesting. Like men in powerful positions, do you? Well, they do say power is an aphrodisiac. How else can you explain all those beautiful, young girls attached to the arm of some short, fat high-flyer (no, it's not always about the money, you cynical thing!). Dating your boss can be very sexy. You can give it lots of 'I'm at your beck and call Mr Big,' as you lean over his impressive desk in your new suit. But keep it quiet for as long as you can. Other women in the office may resent you, and the men will assume you're not good at your job so you're choosing to sleep your way to the top. If possible, I suggest a career move – try a new company where you won't be known as the boss's bird. He can't easily move (and is presumably earning more than you), so it's easier if you get out and about and look for a change. While you are in the same office, don't use your feminine wiles to get ahead at work, only use them for the greater good of the entire team – that is, a new coffee machine, better pension scheme, and so on. Prepare to be gossiped about. Only you know if he's worth it.

Dating a client

The most important thing is to split work from play. Don't tell him company secrets, and don't expect him to be a spy for you. Check with your superior that there are no logical, fair reasons for you to avoid dating a client, and if not go for it – but again, subtly. Don't promise things – in the bedroom or the boardroom – that you can't deliver. Don't tell him secrets about your boss. In fact, don't talk or moan about work at all until you have a secure relationship and a great level of trust. If you can be moved to a different account so your boyfriend is no longer a client that could be a good idea. And don't just talk about work, have fun as well!

How to handle a break-up without breaking down in the office

Sadly the world doesn't stop when your heart does. The first thing you need to do is let your superior know what's happened – not that he or she should excuse you, but it will just give them a heads up on why you might not be your sparkling self for a few weeks. Don't bore everyone in the office. The shoulder-to-cry-on should not be the office gossip; choose your mum or best friend instead.

Avoid drinking too much, or too many late nights trying

to forget the rat. What you need now more than ever is your health and well-being. If you have a few days' holiday left to take, escape and get a change of scene. Spend all weekend crying if it means you're more controlled in the office come Monday. Try to avoid after-work schmoozing and socialising for a while (you might not be too much fun), but when you can feel yourself pulling together, accept a few invitations and get glammed up for them. Don't read your ex's emails or take phone calls in the office. It's too emotional. Save them for home time. Try not to let this failed romance affect your confidence. He must have been an idiot. And remember: every extra day you spend with Mr Wrong is one less day you will spend with your Mr Right ... you *will* feel happy – and treasured – again.

Secrets of Success

◆ As with all your networking endeavours, when dating you should try to be confident. You are brilliant. Any man would be lucky to have you.

◆ Don't be bullied into having a relationship if you can't be bothered with it at the moment. There is no shame in wanting to concentrate on your career. Have a male friend who you can drag along to family events to stop the lesbian rumours if you're concerned. Being single shouldn't stop you from going out and networking – even if you know there will be mostly couples at the event.

◆ Don't be embarrassed about trying out Internet dating – it's a time-saving blessing for many busy career girls. A few of my friends have met – and married – people they've met on the

World Wide Web. Just don't put your phone number or any personal details on your listing.

◆ If good-looking men are expected at a social event later, don't go out beforehand and get nastily drunk or eat garlic/onions/curry.

◆ We've looked at general networking body language earlier – here are some dating tips: you know he likes you if his knees and/or feet are pointing towards you, he stares at your mouth or into your eyes, he laughs at your jokes and listens to your every word. You're in there, honey, if he's blocking you away from other predators or has you pushed up against a wall!

◆ What would a modern girl be without a bit of romance and affection? In your constant bid for worldwide domination and an impressive bank balance, it's OK to forget about your private life for a while ... but don't forget about it for ever. I'd hate you to wake up in a few decades with a fantastic pension, an honorary degree and a mansion – but no one to love who loves you back, or at least without the memories of such to keep you warm at night. Money, networking and your career can't replace a cuddle, a snuggle or a kiss. Don't ever believe it can.

Resources

Catt, Hilton & Scudamore, Patricia: *30 Minutes to Improve Your Networking Skills*, Kogan Page Ltd, 2000.

Darling, Diane: *The Networking Survival Guide: Get the Success You Want by Tapping into the People You Know*, McGraw Hill Higher Education, 2003.

Lindenfeld, Gael and Stuart: *Confident Networking for Career Success and Satisfaction*, Piatkus Books, 2005.

Lowndes, Leil: *How to Talk to Anyone: 92 Little Communication Tricks for Big Success in Relationships*, McGraw Hill Contemporary, 2003.

RoAne, Susan: *How to Work a Room: The Ultimate Guide to Savvy Socializing In-Person and On-Line*, HarperCollins, 2000.

Stone, Carole: *The Ultimate Guide to Successful Networking*, Vermilion, 2004.

Timperley, John: *Network Your Way To Success: Discover the secrets of the world's top connectors*, Piatkus Books, 2002.

Yeung, Rob: *The Rules of Networking*, Cyan Books, 2006.

Index